REVELATION
Explained
by Dr. Bob Beltz

Table of Contents

PART ONE: The Things that Are

PART TWO: The Things that Are to Come

Introduction

I was twenty years old when someone told me Jesus was coming again. I was a brand new believer and the person who informed me of this fact also gave me a book to read. It was Hal Lindsey's *Late Great Planet Earth*. After graduating from college I took a position as a youth pastor at Trinity Evangelical Free Church in Holdrege, Nebraska. It was there that I first tackled the challenge of teaching through the book of Revelation. I'm not sure what our youth group got out of the exercise, but I'm pretty sure I at least drove home the fact that Jesus is coming again.

After serving several years as a youth pastor, my wife and I moved to Denver, Colorado, where I began studies at Denver Seminary (Conservative Baptist Theological Seminary in those days!) I happened to begin classes in January, which meant that the other students had a leg up on me. My very first day in seminary I had a class on the New Testament epistles taught by Dr. Donald Burdick. Dr. Burdick was one of the translators of the New International Version of the Bible. He happened to be beginning this semester in I Thessalonians and as I sat in my desk chair I noticed he had put a timeline of end-times events on the blackboard. As I studied the timeline I noticed that he had put the line for the Rapture of the church in the "wrong" place. Instead of drawing the line at the beginning of the Tribulation, he had placed it at the end of the Tribulation, concurrent with the Second Coming.

I don't know exactly what I was thinking, but in a moment of pure ignorance I raised my hand. When called upon I pointed out his error. There was dead silence in the classroom. That was followed by the first of many times in seminary where a professor absolutely shredded me. On the positive side, I did discover that there was more than one way of understanding the complexity of the end-times.

In the following years I made a number of attempts to teach the book of Revelation. I had the conviction that my students had the right to know what no one had told me before that fateful day in seminary. I taught the book, and when appropriate, explained the various options. The study and research that went into teaching those classes eventually ended up in a book I titled, *How to Survive the End of the World.* That book was published in 1982. It remained relevant over the years due to the fact that I primarily stuck to the text of Revelation rather than giving into whatever the eschatological flavor of the month was. But eventually, it needed an update.

Revelation Explained is that update. I have attempted to revise and enhance the previous work. I have used more relevant examples where appropriate. It also hopefully reflects the thirty-plus years of teaching the Bible I have under my belt since my first efforts at helping men and women understand Revelation. I hope you will find the efforts helpful.

PART ONE
The Things that Are

CHAPTER ONE - *The End of the Beginning*

The revelation of Jesus Christ...(Revelation 1:1).

The end of the world is coming. The only question is when. I imagine this sounds like pessimistic fatalism, or religious fanaticism. It isn't. It is pre-determined realism. The world as we know it is going to end. History is teleological. It is heading somewhere, and the future of the planet is guaranteed.

In the bigger scheme of things, the end of this world is actually a good thing. It is part of a much bigger event that will change the entire universe. But even beyond that, the future of the physical universe is part of a much larger reality that has been playing out in a dimension that is not restricted by time and space. In that reality a conflict has been raging since before the beginning of time and space. The bigger battle in the universe has already been won, and the part planet earth plays in this larger drama is almost over. The end is near.

An End-times Odyssey

The year was 1968. It was a year that defined the times. Bobby Kennedy was assassinated, the war in Vietnam was raging, men were walking on the moon, and the inner cities of America were in a state of racial upheaval. It was the year the Beatles went on the Magical Mystery Tour. It was the age of Woodstock. The turbulence of the moment led to visions of the future ranging from the pessimism of *Clockwork Orange* to the mystical optimism of a film set in the not so distant future: *2001: A Space Odyssey.*

2001: A Space Odyssey was based on Arthur C. Clark's short story, "The Sentinel". Clark collaborated on the screenplay which portrayed Stanley Kubrick's vision of human evolution and the future of humanity using space travel and computers possessing artificial intelligence: ("I wouldn't do that Dave.") It was nearly impossible to watch the film without calculating one's age in the year 2001. It seemed nearly impossible that we would live to see the dawn of a new millennium.

With the transformation of astronaut David Bowman into the Star Child, gazing back at planet Earth, it would seem that Kubrick held an optimistic view of the future. But for most of us, the film was so obscure that we left the theater not sure what to make of what we had just seen.

The same might be said of people who try to understand another wild adventure story. It is not a space odyssey. It is an end-times odyssey. It is found in the last book of the Bible: *Revelation*.

For two millennia the Christian church has asserted that the words of this vision are inspired by God and tell the story of how the world will end. But like Kubrick's film, multitudes come away from reading the book not sure to make of what they have just read. Why is that?

Epistemology is the study of how we know what we know. The study has a great deal of bearing on the Bible. Mankind seeks knowledge in a variety of ways. The most common means of gaining information about the physical world is referred to as the scientific method. Using this method, man observes the world and filters his observations through the grid of his finite reasoning. Theories are formulated, hypothesis are developed and tested, and conclusions are reached. In many areas of life this process is entirely appropriate and has yielded a massive and reliable body of knowledge.

When dealing with the future a certain amount of scientific reasoning can be applied. For instance, we know that at the current rate of abuse the ozone layer protecting the earth's surface from the damaging effects of the sun is being destroyed. Based on the data we can make certain predictions about our environmental future.

We also know that at times past large meteors have struck the surface of the Earth causing cataclysmic outcomes. With a certain degree of probability, we know that a day is coming when Earth will be hit by an asteroid of such magnitude that all life on the planet will be destroyed. Scientists tell us it is not a matter of "if", but "when".

But much of what the future holds is entirely outside the reach of the scientific method. Knowing the ultimate destiny of the planet is not a matter of human reasoning. Science has limitations.

Once you move outside the realm of the scientific, your options concerning information about the future become quite limited. Many people move into the realm of speculation when it comes to the future of humanity. This speculation has produced massive numbers of theories. Some of these theories are optimistic. They project that mankind will conquer the dangers that threaten his extinction and continue to progress toward a more positive future.

Following two World Wars, and the philosophical influence of the nihilistic elite, those that hold these theories have become a dying breed.

Many theories about the future are incredibly pessimistic. The plethora of books and movies portraying dystopian futures speak to the pessimism many hold. Research shows that the percentage of those who believe the future will be worse than the past is significantly higher than the percentage of those with an optimistic outlook. But in the end, both are merely speculative.

But there is another source of information concerning the future. That source is revelation. Revelation in the broader sense refers to something being made known that human reasoning, or the scientific method, cannot know In relationship to the Bible, God reveals who he is, what he thinks, what he has done, and what he is going to do.

More specifically, the book of *Revelation* claims to be an *apocalupsis* from God. The Greek word means an "unveiling". That which cannot be known by normal sources is made known by God. He "unveils" truth.

Revelation contains an unveiling of the future destiny of mankind and planet Earth. These facts cannot be known by human reason or scientific inquiry. They are revelatory in nature.

The human author of *Revelation* did not speculate, nor did he use pure reason to communicate the message of this book. He became a vehicle of divine revelation. He wrote what he saw and heard. In a sense, he is simply our tour guide on our end-times odyssey. The true source of this information is identified in the very first verse of the text. The *Apocalypse* is "the revelation of Jesus Christ" (Rev. 1:1).

Jesus revealed "the things which must soon take place". Through a series of visions Jesus unlocked the mystery of the future. He instructed John to write it all down. John did. Two thousand years later, we not only can study the message, we can watch as the things revealed in it take place all around us.

Meet John

Before we go any further on our end-times odyssey, we should take a few minutes to become acquainted with its human author. In the text of *Revelation*, the author simply identifies himself as "John". The traditional understanding of which "John" wrote the book is John the Apostle.

John was the youngest of the disciples. We have good reason to believe that when John was with Jesus he was only a teenager. By the time John wrote *Revelation* he was at least eighty years old, maybe even into his nineties.

In 70 A.D. the Roman army destroyed the city of Jerusalem. Even after the time of Christ the Jewish people aggressively resisted the Roman occupation of their land. The Romans finally retaliated with force. Under the command of the Roman general Titus, Jerusalem was besieged and destroyed. The temple was burned to the ground and the early church was scattered.

Tradition tells us that following the destruction of Jerusalem, John moved to the city of Ephesus in Asia Minor. In Ephesus John served as a pastor, teacher, prophet, and apostle. He became known as "The Elder".

We believe John received this vision around 95 A.D. A considerable period of time had elapsed between those days when John walked the rugged roads of Galilee with Jesus and the writing of *Revelation*. If we date the book at this time period, we can understand why in the text John identifies himself as a "companion is the suffering…that is ours in Christ Jesus" and the historical situation that led to him being on Patmos.

The Roman general Titus, went on to become the ruler of the Roman Empire. After his death in 81 AD, his brother Domitian became Emperor. He ruled the Empire for fifteen years. During the reign of Domitian the Christians faced tremendous persecution.

Unlike his brother, Domitian demanded to be worshipped as a god. He had himself announced in public as "Our Lord and God Domitian". During his reign every citizen of the empire was required to come before the local magistrate once a year and burn a pinch of incense while confessing, "Caesar is Lord". If a person refused to do so, he was viewed as a political enemy of the Roman Empire. When Christians refused to worship Domitian they were persecuted and subjected to banishment, or even death.

The message of *Revelation* is set against this background. During the time of the ministry of the Apostle Paul, the Roman emperor did not demand Caesar worship. The Roman government, until around 64 A.D., was often a friend of the Gospel. When Paul got in a bind in Jerusalem he appealed to Caesar. Paul viewed the Roman government as a friend to be treated respectfully (see *Romans* chapter 13).

In contrast, by the time John wrote *Revelation*, the government

4

had become Anti-Christ; it was now the "Beast". Christians were not to be in submission to this government when it told them to worship Caesar and deny Jesus.

Patmos was a small rocky island about 40 miles off the coast of Asia Minor. It served as a Roman penal colony where political enemies were banished. Banishment was a severe punishment. It involved the loss of all civil rights, the loss of all personal property, and a life of hard labor in the mines on Patmos. John wrote that he "was on the island of Patmos because of the word of God and the testimony of Jesus," (Rev. I:9).

It was costly to be a Christian in those days. When commanded to confess Caesar as Lord, the faithful Christian would respond, "Jesus is Lord, and there is no other." When John's turn came to burn his incense and make his confession, it was "Goodbye, Ephesus, and Hello, Patmos!"

Signs and Symbols

There is a reason why so many people find *Revelation* so difficult to understand. The message of the book is communicated in a unique literary form. It is a genre that is significantly different than the rest of the documents that make up the New Testament.

In the opening words of *Revelation* we are told that certain facts are going to be "made known" to John. The Greek word translated "made known" (*semeion*) could literally be translated as "to signify". *Revelation* contains a message that is communicated by the use of signs and symbols. These kinds of futuristic messages, communicated in highly symbolic language, are called apocalyptic literature.

Revelation is the only piece of literature in the New Testament that is apocalyptic. There are several examples of the apocalyptic in the Old Testament. Some of Daniel's visions would be considered apocalyptic. Although the visions were highly symbolic in nature, they were fulfilled in specific historic events.

Nebuchadnezzar's vision of the statue, found in *Daniel* chapter two, symbolically represented four coming world empires. As the historic timetable unfolded each of these empires appeared on the stage of world history, exactly as portrayed in the apocalyptic vision. Daniel's vision of the four beasts, found in *Daniel* chapter seven, carried the same message.

The symbols of *Revelation* are like a code that needs to be broken in order to understand the message of the book. John writes of seeing a woman in heaven with the sun, the moon, and the stars all around her. He writes about a dragon flying through the sky, a horde of locusts coming out of a pit, and six-winged beasts surrounding thrones with white-robed elders seated on them.

As we have seen, these things were written during a time when the early Christians were experiencing great persecution at the hands of the Roman Empire. If a Roman soldier read what John had written he probably would have thought John had been out in the sun too long. The soldier didn't have the code to crack the message. But the early Christians had the key to the code.

Of the 404 verses in the book of *Revelation*, over 300 contain allusions or connections to the Old Testament. If the reader knew and understood the Old Testament, they would have a leg up on understand the visionary message. When John said he saw a woman clothed with the sun, the moon, and the twelve stars, Christians would immediately have thought of Joseph's dream in the book of *Genesis*. The woman would have been understood as a symbol of the people of God. To break the code, you needed to know the Old Testament.

The Message

The message of the book of *Revelation* is summarized in the very first chapter. The seventh verse of that chapter reads:

Look, he is coming with the clouds,
and every eye will see him,
even those who pierced him:
and all the peoples of the earth
will mourn because of him.
So shall it be! Amen.

The primary message of *Revelation* is that Jesus Christ is returning to planet Earth. This is the bottom line of human history. It was a message intended to encourage suffering believers in John's day. It is a message intended to motivate and encourage believing men and women in the days in which we live.

The message is rooted in two Old Testament prophecies. *Zechariah* 12:10 reads:

And I will pour out on the house of David and the inhabitants of

6

Jerusalem a spirit of grace and supplication. They will look on me, the one they have pierced, and they will mourn for him as one mourns for an only child..."

The second prophecy is from the book of *Daniel*. It reads:

In my vision at night I looked and there before me was one like a Son of Man, coming with the clouds of heaven, (Daniel 7:13).

These passages predict the coming of the kingdom of God and its final victory over every kingdom man has established. The manner in which these two texts are woven together, and the context and content of the prophesies in their original setting, summarize every theme that is contained in the apocalyptic vision of John. Here is the message of *Revelation:*

1. Jesus Christ is coming again.
2. At his coming, the nations will be judged.
3. The Kingdom of Man will be crushed.
4. The Kingdom of God will be established as an everlasting kingdom.

God wins! That is the message of the book. It is a message that will take us on a spiritual odyssey and help us learn how to live in the end-times.

CHAPTER TWO - *The Odyssey Begins*

I was in the Spirit on the Lord's Day, (Revelation 1:10).

In the Spirit

You have probably heard the old expression, "It's not what you know, but who you know that counts." When it comes to understand something of our future destiny this statement is definitely true. Our future destiny is intimately linked to our relationship with the author of the future. Thus, it seems fitting that John's odyssey began with an incredible encounter with Jesus Christ.

It is probably difficult for most of us to put ourselves in John's shoes at the time he had this experience. We have seen something of the historical circumstances that surrounded the writing of *Revelation* in the last chapter.

John wrote that he was a fellow sufferer in the tribulation that his first century audience was experiencing. Stripped of position and possessions, and having seen many good friends lost to the sword of Domitian, John must have had times when he questioned whether the claims of Jesus, some sixty years earlier, were really true.

Was all authority on heaven and earth truly vested in the risen Christ? If so, why were times so incredibly difficult for believers? Yet, even in the midst of what was perhaps the most difficult times of his life we are given a glimpse of John's spiritual condition and circumstances which made his physical difficulties bearable.

John wrote that he was " in the Spirit, on the Lord's Day" (Rev. 1:10). This is the first recorded use of the term "the Lord's Day" to refer to the Christian day of worship. Within the Roman Empire one day of the week was designated as the Lord's Day or the Emperor's day. It was so designated because this was the day of the week that the current emperor ascended the throne of Rome and began his rule.

Most of the early followers of Christ were Jewish by background. The Jewish day of worship was called the Sabbath. On our calendars the Sabbath falls on Saturday. Jesus Christ rose from the grave on the fist day of the week; i.e., Sunday. Since in the eyes of the church this was the day that the true ruler ascended the ultimate throne they began to meet early on Sunday morning to worship Christ. They began to refer to Sunday as the Lord's Day.

Even in exile it is obvious that John set this time aside to worship the Lord because he tells us that he was "in the Spirit". There are two possibilities of what this phrase means. On the one hand John might simply be making the observation that he was living under the dominant influence of the Holy Spirit. To be in the Spirit in this sense is the intended normative daily experience of the practicing Christian.

The other possibility is that John was an extraordinary experience of spiritual ecstasy like the Old Testament prophets. My own hunch is that the phrase reflects both of these realities.

In the darkest moment of his life, God intervened in John's life and enabled John to experience the reality of the unseen spiritual realm. In this altered state of spiritual consciousness, John heard a voice and turned to see who was speaking to him.

The Risen Christ

John wrote that he heard behind him a loud voice which sounded like a trumpet, (Rev. 1:10). When he turned to see the source of this voice he was justifiably overwhelmed. The Apostle sees the exalted and glorified Christ.

Some sixty years had elapsed since John last saw Jesus. During the time of Christ's earthly ministry they shared a relationship that was so intimate that John often referred to himself as "the disciple whom Jesus loved."

When Christ shared the Passover meal with his disciples in the Upper Room, John reclined with his head on Jesus' breast. This posture revealed the closest possible kind of friendship. The Jesus John now sees is quite different from the Jesus of those days.

John now sees Jesus as he is: risen, exalted, and glorified. John attempted to describe what he saw by using a series of phrases borrowed from Old Testament prophesy. He said he saw a man standing in the midst of seven golden lampstands, (Rev. 1:12). This "man" is Jesus Christ. John identifies ten characteristics of Jesus as revealed in this vision.

Characteristic One: *Like a Son of Man.*

The first characteristic of Christ in this glorified state is that to John he appeared to be "like a Son of Man". "Son of Man" was one of the Old Testament titles for the coming Messiah and Savior of the Jewish people.

In the Old Testament book of *Daniel*, chapter 7, Daniel experienced a vision that contained many similarities to John's vision on Patmos. Daniel's vision involved the final judgment of the kingdoms of men and the establishment of the Kingdom of God in its final form. In the text Daniel says,

I saw in the night visions and behold, with the clouds of heaven there came one like a Son of Man, and he came to the Ancient of Days and was presented before him. And to him was given dominion and glory and a kingdom."

This is the same passage of Scripture quoted by Jesus on the Mount of Olives when he prophesied about his second coming (see Matthew 24). The "Son of Man" of Daniel's vision now stands before John on the island of Patmos. He is the returning Messianic King of the coming eternal kingdom of God.

Characteristic Two: *Dressed in a robe reaching down to his feet.*

This type of robe was the traditional dress of both a Jewish priest and judge. The risen Christ is both. He is the great High Priest over the church. But, he is also the judge of the church and the world. In relationship to the church this is not a judgment of punishment.
Jesus died to free the church from this destiny. His judgment is a refining judgment intended to restore the church to the purity he desires and demands.

It is such a refining judgment that is about to be executed in the messages he will send to the seven churches of Asia Minor. In relationship to the world, he is the one who will sit on a great white throne judging the nations. We will address this judgment when we get to chapter twenty.

Characteristic Three: *With a golden sash around the chest.*

Christ's robe is secured by a golden sash. In John's day the sash was a symbol of authority. Gold was a symbol of deity. One of the main themes of the apocalyptic vision of *Revelation* is the deity of Christ. His deity is the source of his authority to judge.

11

Characteristic Four: *His head and hair were white like wool.*

In Daniel's vision it was the Ancient of Days, God the Father, who was described as having hair white like wool. This description of Christ's appearance is one of many instances in *Revelation* where an attribute of God the Father is ascribed to Christ, the Son. The white symbolizes the purity and holiness of God. White hair was a symbol of age, which in John's day was viewed as a mark of maturity and wisdom. These symbols tell us something of the character of Christ's refining judgment; it is holy, pure, wise, and discerning.

Characteristic Five: *His eyes were like blazing fire.*

In the tenth chapter of *Daniel*, Daniel has an encounter with an angelic being that many scholars believe was an Old Testament appearance of Christ, called a Christophany. This "man", Daniel tells us, had "eyes like blazing torches", (Daniel 10:6). Fire is another symbol of refining judgment. We are told in Hebrews 4:13 that nothing is hidden from him, but that everything is "laid bare before the eyes of him to whom we must give account." It will be the very gaze of Christ that penetrates the life of the churches, the hearts of believers, and the conduct of the world he loves.

Characteristic Six: *His feet were like bronze glowing in a furnace.*

Bronze is another Old Testament image that has a relationship to the concept of judgment. It was at the bronze altar that the nation of Israel brought it's sacrifices as a substitute for the judgment of God. When Israel was in the wilderness Moses was instructed to raise a bronze serpent on a pole as a means of escaping the judgment of God. Bronze or brass thus became a symbol of judgment.

The brass feet take on more significance later in the book of *Revelation* when the feet of Jesus Christ trample out "the wine press of the wrath of God" (Rev. 19:15). The fact that these bronze feet are glowing shows us that judgment is immanent.

Characteristic Seven: *His voice was like the sound of rushing waters.*

In the prophesy of Ezekiel, the prophet describes the return of the glory of the Lord to the restored millennial temple of Israel. Ezekiel describes the voice of God by saying it was like the sound of rushing waters. Here it is the voice of Christ that is described this way.

This symbol speaks of the awesome majesty and power of the Word of Christ. Later, the instrument of judgment in both the church and the world is the Word of God.

Characteristic Eight: *In his right hand he held seven stars.*

This is one of the few symbols in *Revelation* that Christ himself explains. In the twentieth verse of this first chapter Jesus tells John that the stars are the "angels" of the seven churches. The word "angel" literally means "messenger". In the context of *Revelation* it appears to refer to the men vested with the authority or responsibility for the local churches.

The right hand is the place of supreme authority. This image pictures Christ as the ultimate authority over the church. The leaders of the church ultimately answer to him. In the following chapters we will see that he will hold the "angels" responsible for the spiritual condition of the churches he addresses.

Characteristic Nine: *Out of his mouth came a sharp double-edged sword.*

The sword is a vivid image that is referred to in several New Testament texts as a symbol of the Word of God. *Hebrews* 4:13 states that "the Word of God is living and active; sharper than any two-edged sword". In *Ephesians* chapter six, the Apostle Paul describes the Word as "the sword of the Spirit", (Eph. 6:17). The instrument of Christ's refining judgment in the church and the world is, and will be, his Word.

The *Hebrews* text tells us that the function of the Word as a sword is to divide and judge the thoughts and intentions of the heart. When we explore the messages Jesus addresses to the seven churches of chapters two and three we will discover that this is exactly what Christ does.

Characteristic Ten: *His face was like the sun shining in all its brilliance.*

13

The tenth and final characteristic of the glorified Christ is the radiance of his face. When Daniel saw the Angel of the Lord he said that his face was like lightning (Daniel 10:6). Both descriptions reflect the glory of the face of God reflected in the face of Christ. This is the glory that was veiled during the years of Jesus' incarnation which is now unveiled forever.

Disciple down!

I'm sure that reading this description, and even trying to explain the meaning of these ten characteristics, falls far short of the impact this experience had on John. Every characteristic is described by using the word "like". This vision was not like anything John had ever seen. At best he gives us hints of what he saw. The best understanding of this vision comes by looking at John's response to it.

John tells us that he fell at Christ's feet as though dead. He was overwhelmed and properly terrified. This was not Jesus his old friend. This was Christ; the risen, exalted, and glorified Lord! As John was lying on the ground, Jesus reached out and touched him. He said to John:

Do not be afraid. I am the First and the Last. I am the Living One; I was dead, and now look, I am alive for ever and ever! And I hold the keys of death and Hades, (Revelation 10:17-18).

This is the key to understanding the future. If Christ is not risen from the dead, and glorified with the glory he had with the Father from before the foundation of the world, then the future of humanity hangs in the balance.

But, if Jesus Christ is not only risen, but also glorified, then he is not only the Lord of the Church; he is the Lord of the future, also. This is exactly the message of *Revelation*!

CHAPTER THREE - *Letters to the Churches (pt.1)*

To the messenger of the church in Ephesus write: (Rev. 2:1).

A Promise

Before we get into the letters to the seven churches, I wanted to point out that *Revelation* is the only book in the New Testament that carries a special promise with it. In the prologue to the book John wrote:

Blessed is the one who reads aloud the words of this prophecy, and blessed are those who hear it and take to heart what is written in it, because the time is near, (Rev. 1:3).

Taking time to read the Bible is one of the foundational spiritual disciplines of the spiritual life. It is like spiritual food in the same way prayer is like spiritual air. In order to thrive in our relationship with Jesus, we need to spend consistent time reading the Bible and connecting with God in prayer.

But there is a special promise for those who read *Revelation* and "take to heart what is written in it". This makes it even more ironic, and tragic, that so many people avoid the book due to an inability to understand it. But all this is going to change for you, because you are now going to understand the book and read it. So I trust that as we move through *Revelation*, you will be blessed!

Love Letters

On Patmos, the risen Christ gave John a commission. Two times he instructed John to "write". He first told him to "write on a scroll what you see and send it to the seven churches," (Rev. 1:11). Shorty after this instruction, he again told John to "write". This time he told John to write three specific things to these churches. He told him to write "what you have seen, the things that are, and the things that will take place after these things," (Rev. 1:19).

In 96 AD, Domitian was assassinated. The Roman Senate (which probably played no small role in getting rid of Domitian!) made an elderly statesman by the name of Marcus Nerva the new emperor. He was the first Roman emperor to be elected by the Senate. Under the leadership of Nerva and the Roman Senate, many of Domitian's autocratic policies were reversed. Nerva did not demand worship. He didn't believe he was a god. Those who had been exiled were allowed to return home. John headed back to Ephesus.

Back in Ephesus, probably around 97 AD, John did exactly what Jesus had told him to do. He wrote. In the last chapter we looked at the encounter John had with the glorified Christ. We know the details of this encounter because John wrote "what he had seen".

In chapters two and three of *Revelation*, you will find seven letters, dictated by Jesus, to seven churches in the province of Asia Minor. These letters comprise what Jesus referred to as "the things that are."

Finally, in chapters four through twenty-two, John will write the vision of the future he received on Patmos. These are "the things that will take place after these things." Although many people think of *Revelation* as a book about the future, the seven letters contained in chapters two and three contain some of the most important material in the book. The messages of these letters are as relevant today as they were when John wrote what Jesus dictated.

Ephesus: the church that had lost its first love.

The Roman province of Asia occupied the land that today is known as Turkey. There were more than seven churches in this province. The question that we might ask is whether or not there was a particular reason why Jesus picked these seven churches to address.

Numbers play an important role in apocalyptic literature. Seven was a number that symolized wholeness or completeness. Since Jesus picked seven churches, it is safe to assume that he intended these messages to be read by more than just these specific churches. Throughout history, the seven churches have been seen as representing the whole church. Because of this, each letter has a number of applications.

In their historic context, these letters were written to seven literal churches of John's day. Certain conditions existed in each of these churches that prompted Jesus to address a message to them. There were probably other churches at the time of John's writing that were characterized by the same realities. In this case, the letters carried a message of "if the shoe fits, wear it!"

There is also a sense in which these seven churches reflect types of churches that have existed in every generation. The same "shoe fitting" principle applies. Some interpreters have suggested that the seven churches are representative of eras in church history. It takes some stretching to see how this fits, but there are some interesting parallels between the messages and the unfolding history of the Church.

There is also a sense in which the issues addressed in each letter also apply to seven types of people who have existed in every generation. As such we can analyze the messages and seek to use the information as a stimulus for our own personal spiritual growth.

The first of these seven messages is addressed to the church in the city of Ephesus. This was once the greatest city in all of Asia Minor. It had an excellent harbor and was located on the land bridge that linked Europe to the Orient. By the time *Revelation* was written the city was in state of economic decline. But during this period of economic decline it had become the spiritual epicenter of the entire province of Asia Minor.

The message Jesus gave was addressed to "the angel of the church in Ephesus," (Rev. 2:1). Each of the seven letters begins with this kind of commission. The word that is usually translated "angel" in our English bibles literally means "messenger". There is some debate about whether the letters are being written to a literal angel who has some kind of spiritual connection to the individual churches, or whether in symbolic language the "messenger" is the human authority that has spiritual responsibility for the church. I lean toward this interpretation. Otherwise there would be no need to write an actual letter and deliver it to an actual church.

Each letter also contains a reference by Jesus to one of the characteristics revealed about him in the vision of chapter one. Here he notes he is the one who walks among the seven golden lampstands and holds the seven stars. Jesus is Lord of the Church and Lord over the leaders of the Church.

The third element all the letters contain is some kind of commendation from Jesus about the good that is taking place in the individual churches. In its historic context, Christ commended the men and women of the church in Ephesus for five positive qualities:

1. Jesus told John to write that he knew of the church's hard work and toil, (vs. 2). This was a church that took the call to ministry

and service seriously and labored at their task with everything they had.

2. He also commended them for their stand on moral and ethical issues by acknowledging that they "can't tolerate wicked men" (vs. 2). Theologically, this was a church that was doctrinally sound and orthodox. In his earlier letter (I John), John had counseled the churches of Asia Minor to "test the spirits", (I John 4:1). By this time in church history there were already many false teachers on the loose. Ephesus had "tested the spirits" and exposed those who claimed to be apostles but were not (vs. 2).

This doctrinal stability was matched with a spirit of steadfastness. Jesus commended them that they had endured hardship and persevered, (vs. 3). A few verses later he also acknowledged their hatred of the practice of the Nicolaitans, (vs. 6).

Tradition identifies the Nicolaitans as a heretical sect that arose in the early church. The most consistent research would indicate that the sect taught a distorted doctrine of grace that led to immorality under the guise of grace. Since the Ephesians hated this doctrine, it would be safe to assume that they had a measure of moral purity in behavior that was reflected in their attitude toward this cult.

When you put all these characteristics together you can see that many good things were happening in the life of the church in Ephesus. Unfortunately, there was one major problem that overshadowed all that was good.

As well as commendation, all the letters also contain critique from Jesus regarding anything in the life of the church that displeased him. Even with everything good taking place in Ephesus, they had a problem. Jesus said that they had "lost their first love."

The church was in its second generation. Forty years had passed since Paul brought the good news of Jesus to Ephesus. By the time John wrote *Revelation*, their orthodoxy had become a dead orthodoxy. Their passion for loving Christ had either been neglected or marginalized. They had drifted from the most important part of the Christian life: love of Jesus.

The primary purpose of life is to love God and to love one another. When Jesus designed the church, he intended it to be a gathering of people who loved him and who loved each other. Unfortunately, the human tendency is to lose sight of the forest for the trees. In Ephesus, the second generation of believers were doing all the right things, but without the one characteristic that gave all they did true meaning and authenticity.

In each of the seven letters, Jesus follows his critique with a instructions on how to correct the problem. In Ephesus, this correction involved the church remembering what things were like in the days when love for Christ was their highest priority.

I believe the contemporary way of articulating this correction would be to challenge us to keep Christ first. Nothing is an acceptable substitute for the priority of our relationship with God. If we lose this priority in our life, our spiritual life will degenerate into a lifeless religiosity.

The correction for the Ephesians also included a change of attitude. Jesus told them to repent. The essence of this word in the original language was a change of mind that leads to a change of direction. You can think of it as walking in one direction, and then realizing you are heading the wrong way. At that point you have a decision to make. You can keep on your current trajectory, or you can stop and make a mid-course correction. True repentance occurs when a change is made and we head straight toward God. Think of it as a spiritual "alignment".

The final elements you will find in each letter are a call to hear what Jesus has said (via the letter), and a challenge with a promise he makes to those who "overcome". An "overcomer" is a church or individual who heeds the message and makes the appropriate changes. The promises Jesus gives are so amazing that the impact of the promise should motivate obedience.

The promise to the church in Ephesus was a promise of access to the Tree of Life and entrance into Paradise. Everything that Adam lost in the Garden of Eden will be made available again to the man or woman who loves Jesus, and keeps him first in their lives. What could be more important?

To the messenger of the church in Smyrna write: (Rev. 2:8).

The second church to which Christ addressed a letter was located in the city of Smyrna. Of all the cities to which letters were addressed, Smyrna was probably the most renowned and beautiful. It was called "The Crown Jewel of Asia".

This was a city known for its economic prominence. Along with having a natural harbor, it sat on the major trade route from Rome to Persia. All of the trade from East to West passed through the city of Smyrna.

The economy of the city was heavily influenced by its trade guilds. These were similar to our modern labor unions. We are going to see why that was significant when we focus on the problems the church in Smyrna was facing.

This was also a city known for its architectural beauty. As trade flourished, a great deal of money went into building ornate structures within the city.

Smyrna was the leading Roman city in Asia Minor and the headquarters of the Roman government. It was a center of political prominence and also a city of tremendous religious preeminence.

Many different gods were worshiped in Smyrna. It was the first city in Asia Minor to have a temple dedicated to Caesar. Consequently, it became a center of the most problematic religious issue facing the early church: Caesar worship.

Smyrna also had a large and influential Jewish population that worked in close cooperation with the Roman authorities. The Jews had contributed great amounts of money to the beautification of the city. By the end of the first century, many of the problems the Christians in Smyrna faced came from the antagonism of the Jewish population.

The First and the Last

In this letter, the part of Jesus' description from chapter one that is highlighted is his eternal nature and his resurrection. Jesus told John to write, "These are the words of him who is the First and the Last, who died and came to life again," (Rev. 2:8).

This little phrase, "the First and the Last," is drawn from the Old Testament book of *Isaiah*. On numerous occasions in *Isaiah*, God referred to himself by using the title "The First and the Last."

In *Isaiah* 44:6, we read:

This is what the Lord says, Israel's King and Redeemer, the Lord Almighty. I am the First and I am the Last, apart from me there is no God.

Now, in *Revelation*, Jesus Christ uses this same phrase to identify himself. A strong emphasis upon the deity of Jesus Christ is prominent throughout *Revelation*. You will see many times where Christ is identified with God by taking an Old Testament statement about *YHWH* and applying it to Jesus Christ.

Throughout this passage in *Isaiah*, the phrase "the First and Last" emphasizes the eternal nature of God and his sovereign ability, even in the midst of difficulties, to accomplish his purposes.

When Isaiah was writing, the nation of Israel had been carried into captivity to Babylon. Jerusalem had been pillaged, the Temple destroyed, and everything in which the people had placed their hopes crushed. God, through Isaiah, told Israel the reason for what had happened. In *Isaiah* 48:10, the prophet writes the words of God to Israel:

See, I have refined you, though not as silver; I have tested you in the furnace of affliction. For my own sake I do this. How can I let myself be defamed? I will not yield my glory to another.

God told Israel that the experiences they had been through were meant to be refining experiences. Even in the midst of their suffering and affliction, God's purposes were being accomplished. When God calls himself "the First and the Last", he is saying that he is the one who knows the beginning from the end. He was there in the beginning; he will be there in the end. When history as we know it ends, we will see that God's plans have been accomplished, even in the midst of suffering and difficulty.

To the church at Smyrna, this was extremely important. Of all the churches in the book of *Revelation*, none was under greater persecution than the church in the city of Smyrna. To a church that was facing persecution for its faith, Jesus Christ revealed Himself as "the First and the Last". He was saying to them, "I am still in control of your situation."

22

Tough times at Smyrna

In this letter Jesus commended the church in Smyrna with these words: "I know your afflictions and your poverty--yet you are rich! I know the slander of those who say they are Jews and are not, but are a synagogue of Satan," (Rev. 2:9).

When Jesus says, "I know your afflictions" He uses the Greek word, *thlipsis*. This word can be translated "suffering", "affliction", or "tribulation". The church in Smyrna was particularly subject to tribulation for their belief in Jesus Christ. Mobs attacked and wrecked their homes, dragged off believers, beat them, threw them into prison, and even put some to death.

At the time John wrote *Revelation,* one of his personal disciples was the leader of the church of Smyrna. His name was Polycarp. In his history of the early church, Eusebius tells us that in 155 A.D., when Polycarp was an old man, he was martyred for his faith.

Eusebius gives extensive details about this incident. He writes that the crowds at Smyrna were at the public games, and began to chant, "Away with the atheists, let Polycarp be searched for." Christians in those days were known as atheists, because they refused to worship Caesar.

The night before he was put to death, Eusebius writes that Polycarp had a dream in which he saw himself sleeping on a burning pillow. He went to the people in his church and told them that God had revealed to him that he must be burned alive for his faith.

The next day when Roman soldiers came to arrest Polycarp, he had prepared a meal for them. He told his disciples to serve the men who had come to take him to his death. Eusebius again tells us that as Polycarp entered the arena to be martyred, a voice came from heaven and said, "Be strong, Polycarp, and play the man."

In the arena, the Roman magistrate gave him a final choice. Either he could curse the name of Christ and sacrifice to Caesar, or be put to death. His response was, "Eighty and six years I have served him, and He has done me no wrong. How can I blaspheme my king who saved me?"

Again, the magistrate threatened him and told him that if he did not curse the name of Christ and sacrifice to Caesar, he would be burned at the stake. Polycarp responded, "You threaten me with the fire that burns for a time and is quickly quenched, for you do not know the fire that awaits the wicked in the judgment to come and in everlasting punishment. Why are you waiting? Come do what you will."

The townspeople brought burning embers to set Polycarp on fire. The Jews were so antagonistic that even though the day was the Sabbath, they violated the Law by carrying the wood to the arena to fuel the fire to burn Polycarp. As they were getting ready to bind him to the stake, Polycarp said,

"Leave me as I am, for he who gives me power to endure the fire will grant me to remain in the flames unmoved, even without the security you will give by the ropes."

As the fire was kindled, Polycarp prayed,

O Lord God Almighty, father of your beloved and blessed child Jesus Christ, through whom we have received full knowledge of you; God of angels and powers and of all creation, and of the whole family of the righteous who live before you; I bless you, that you have granted unto me this day and hour that I may share among the number of the martyrs in the cup of thy Christ, for the resurrection to eternal life, both of soul and body, in the immortality of the Holy Spirit. And may I today be received among them before you as a rich and acceptable sacrifice, as you, the
God without falsehood and of truth have prepared beforehand, and shown forth and fulfilled. For this reason, through the eternal and heavenly high priest Jesus Christ, your beloved child, through whom be glory to you, with him and the Holy Spirit, both now and for the ages that are to come. Amen.

Tradition tells us that when the flames began to surround Polycarp he began to sing. One story reports that he was supernaturally protected and would not burn. A Roman soldier, seeing what was happening, thrust his spear into Polycarp and killed him. Later tradition reports that the smell of his dead, burning body had the fragrance of flowers rather than the stench of burning flesh.

Polycarp's story represents the kind of persecution the church at Smyrna was experiencing at the time John wrote *Revelation*. It was a church in which it cost many their lives to be faithful to their commitment to Jesus Christ.

True Riches

In the letter, Jesus went on to say, "I know your poverty." There are two Greek words that communicate the idea of poverty. The first is the word *penia*. This word was used of someone who was poor and possessed nothing superfluous. All they had were the bare essentials to survive day-to-day. The other Greek word that is translated "poor" in the Bible is the word *ptocheia*. Unlike the poverty of a person who had nothing superfluous, this word spoke of the man or woman who had nothing at all.

The word *ptocheia* is used here to speak of the church at Smyrna. These Christians were living in abject poverty.

Remember that Smyrna was a city whose economy was heavily influenced by trade guilds. In order to make a living in a city like Smyrna, a man had to belong to one of these guilds.

Every trade guild had its own patron deity. To belong to a trade guild, a man was required to sacrifice to the deity of that trade guild. When Christians refused to sacrifice to these deities they were boycotted and often forced out of business.

The result was that the church in Smyrna was experiencing abject poverty and its members were dependent upon one another for their survival. When they said the Lord's Prayer, "Give us this day our daily bread", that is exactly what they were praying for. Paradoxically, to a church in such a difficult situation, Jesus Christ says, "But you are rich."

Compare this statement with what Christ will say to the church at Laodicea in the next chapter of *Revelation*. The church in Laodicea was a very wealthy church. It was not facing the same problems as the church in Smyrna.

Jesus told John to write to the Laodiceans, "You say, 'I am rich, I have acquired wealth and do not need a thing', but you do not realize that you are wretched, pitiful, poor, blind and naked," (Rev. 3:17). What a contrast! The church that had nothing materially was rich spiritually. On the other hand, the church that was rich in material things was spiritually poverty-stricken!

Even in the midst of their poverty, the church at Smyrna was enjoying spiritual riches. They were experiencing the joy, peace, happiness, and contentment that come from a vital relationship with Jesus Christ. Church historians have made an interesting observation. They tell us that the churches of the first three centuries were marked by material poverty and spiritual power, while the churches of the last three centuries have been marked by material wealth and spiritual weakness.

Apparently, it is easy for a church to become affluent materially yet poverty-stricken spiritually. Scripturally, wealth does not consist in the abundance of our possessions, but in the simplicity of our desires. The church at Smyrna had true wealth. They were in touch with God's presence in a way that the other churches were not. Through their poverty they had become rich.

The Synagogue of Satan

Christ continued his commendation by saying, "I know the slander of those who say they are Jews and are not, but are a synagogue of Satan," (Rev. 2:9).

The Jews in Smyrna created tremendous problems for the Christians. There were six issues that were turned into slander against the Christians. The Jewish community in Smyrna seemed to have been behind the promotion these slanders.

The first slander was that the Christians were cannibals. People outside of the church heard about these people who were eating someone's body and drinking his blood, and they accused them of being cannibals!

The second slander they were accused of was having sexual orgies. The Christians had a communal meal they called the "Love Feast". It is possible that this was the way they celebrated sharing the Lord's Supper. When the Greeks and Romans heard about love feasts, their immediate reaction was to identify these love feasts as sexual orgies.

Christians were slandered as being anti-family. Sometimes, when one member of the family came to faith in Jesus it caused division within the family. Outsiders also misunderstood the teaching of Christ when He said, "If anyone loves brother or sister, father or mother more than me, he is not worthy of me."

Christians were called atheists because of the fact that they would not engage in the worship of idols. They were accused of being politically disloyal because they would not sacrifice to Caesar. They were accused of being incendiaries because they always talked about the end of the world in terms of a burning fire. All of these slanders were levied against the church.

The same Jews who slandered and pressured the Christians referred to themselves as "the synagogue of God". Jesus turned that claim around and called them "a synagogue of Satan, "(Rev. 2:9). Jesus also said that they were not even Jews.

The New Testament teaches that being truly Jewish is an inward matter, not simply a matter of physical descent. A true Jew is the person who has been circumcised in his heart, and is responsive to God. That kind of person would manifest God's love in their lives, not spread slander that further exacerbated the difficulties the church was already facing.

No Critique

The church in Smyrna is one of two churches about which Jesus Christ has nothing negative to say. He sends no message of critique. . The church in Smyrna had been tempered by the tribulation they experienced. As a result, there was no critique or correction addressed to the church.

There is a refining power in persecution. In James, chapter one, we are told that testing produces endurance. In I Peter, chapter one, Peter wrote concerning trials: "These have come so that your faith--of greater worth than gold, which perishes even though refined by fire--may be proved genuine," (I Peter 1:7). Testing purifies the church. God refines His people in the furnace of affliction.

Rather than correction, Jesus gave the church counsel about what was about to happen in Smyrna. He told them not be afraid. He warned them, "I tell you that the devil will put some of you in prison to test you, and you will suffer persecution for ten days," (Rev. 2:10).

There are two possibilities of what Christ means here. One is that the local church was about to face a short time of intense persecution. The other is that Christ was symbolically prophesying ten periods of persecution that the church as a whole was going to experience. Some have suggested this statement is alluding to ten Roman emperors who subsequently persecuted the church.

The Crown of Life

Jesus challenged the church to, "Be faithful, even to the point of death," (Rev. 2:10). He promised that if they were, he would give them "the crown of life", (Revelation 2:10).

What is the crown of life? "Crown," in Greek is the word *stephanos*. The *stephanos* was the victor's crown. It often was a laurel wreath given to the athlete who was victorious in the ancient games. It would have been the equivalent of our Olympic gold medal.

The *stephanos* was a perishable crown. But the crown, or the reward that Christ gives, is not. It is a "crown of life". This verse could be translated, "To him who overcomes, I will give the crown *which is* life. The one who is faithful to the point of death will receive the reward of eternal life.

Jesus also promised that the one who is faithful, even to the point of death, will avoid the judgment that is coming when he returns. Later in the book we will see exactly what the words "the second death" mean. For now, he wanted the believers in Smyrna to know they had nothing to fear when that judgment came. They had been faithful!

To the angel of the church in Pergamum write: (Rev. 2:18).

The third of the seven letters Jesus dictated to John was addressed to the church in the city of Pergamum. In this letter, Jesus referred to Pergamum as "the city where Satan has his throne". Historically, Pergamum was one of the greatest cities of Asia Minor. It had been the capital of Asia during the Greek period, and remained the capital in the early years of the Roman period. Pergamum was not a commercial center, but it was a great political and cultural center. It was the home of the second largest library in the Roman Empire after Alexandria.

Even more significant to *Revelation*, Pergamum was a religious center. Some scholars believe it was this characteristic that led Jesus to call it the city where Satan had his throne. On the acropolis at Pergamum stood a massive, forty-foot altar dedicated to the Greek god Zeus. You can see an exact replica of this altar in the Pergamum Museum in Berlin. The altar resembled a giant throne. Some scholars suggest that Zeus, the chief of the Greek pantheon of gods, epitomized pagan religion. Jesus viewed pagan religion as satanic because it led people away from the truth. The age of political correctness had not yet arrived.

Pergamum was also a center of the cult of Asclepius. Asclepius was the Greek god of healing. This god was called "*Asclepius Soter*", meaning "Asclepius the Savior". To a Christian, calling anyone other than Jesus "savior" was abhorrent. The symbol of the cult was a serpent. Again, in Christian theology, the serpent was a symbol of Satan.

Finally, Pergamum was the Roman administrative center of Asia Minor. During the time the Roman Proconsul of Asia resided here, he possessed what was called "the right of the sword". This gave him the authority to execute anyone who refused to worship Caesar. The early church also viewed Caesar worship as demonic. If you put all these elements together, you can see why Jesus would call Pergamum "the city where Satan has his throne".

The Sword of the Spirit

These are the words of him who has the sharp, double-edged sword, (Rev. 2:12).

In this letter, Jesus identified himself as "the one who has the sharp, double-edged sword". In the vision of Jesus in chapter one, John saw a sharp, double-edged sword coming out of Christ's mouth. I can assure you that the exalted and glorified Christ was not walking around with a literal sword coming out of his mouth. The meaning of this symbol can be found in both the epistle to the *Hebrews*, and Paul's letter to the church at Ephesus. The author of *Hebrews* (possibly Paul) wrote, "the Word of God is living and active, and sharper than a double-edged sword," (Hebrews 4:12). In *Ephesians*, Paul called the Word of God the "sword of the Spirit", (Eph. 6:17). When Jesus speaks, what comes from his mouth is the Word of God.

In the Greek language there are two different words that are translated "sword". One is the word, *macharia*. This was a short, dagger-like weapon used by the Roman army in hand-to-hand warfare. It would have been the instrument used by the Roman proconsul when he exercised "the right of the sword". This sword would symbolize Rome's power over physical life and death.

The other word translated "sword" is the word *rhomphaia*. The *rhomphaia* was the large sword that was used in open combat. This is the word that appears in our text. Jesus is the one who wields the *rhomphaia*. The Romans held in their hands the power of physical life and death. But Jesus holds in his hands the power of eternal life and death!

When Jesus enters into combat for the truth, it is the Word of God that is his weapon. He combats error with Truth (with a capital "T"). When a church compromises the truth, Jesus confronts that church with the sword of the Spirit: the Word of God. Such was the case in what Jesus had John write to the church in Pergamum.

Some Good in Pergamum

I know where you live, where Satan has his throne, yet you remain true to my name, (Rev. 2:13).

The commendation Jesus sent to this church was similar to what he commended the church in Smyrna for. He said that even in the midst of the city where Satan had such a presence, they had remained true to their faith in Jesus. The literal rendering of the text would be "you hold fast my name" and "you do not deny my faith". The two go hand in hand.

To "hold fast" means "to hold forcefully", "to refuse to let go", or "to be unwilling to discard". The grammar of the passage indicates a degree of tenacity in not denying the name of Jesus. Jesus intensified this further by adding, "you do not deny my faith". In a city where Caesar worship was widespread, the believers in Pergamum would not deny, "Jesus is Lord". They would not worship Caesar. This was pleasing to Jesus.

To illustrate his commendation, Jesus referred to an incident involving one of their own. He mentions Antipas being put to death in Pergamum. Antipas had been appointed the Bishop of Pergamum by John. He faced a situation very similar to the one Polycarp faced in Smyrna. He was publicly threatened with death if he did not deny Christ and worship Caesar. Tradition tells us that his response was, "Jesus is Lord, and there is no other". In 92 AD, the Romans put him to death by placing him inside a brass bull and roasting him to death. Jesus called him "my faithful witness".

Even in the face of such extreme persecution, the church in Pergamum remained faithful. They met the external threat of persecution. But they had problems internally.

Problems in Pergamum

Nevertheless, I have a few things against you: (Rev. 2:14).

When persecution fails to destroy the church, the enemy turns to other tactics. Persecution has often been a motivator in church history that accelerated the spread of the gospel. The first three centuries of church history were marked by intense persecution. They were also the three most productive centuries in terms of the spread of the message of Jesus and the planting of new churches.

A much worse enemy of the church was false teaching and compromise. It weakened the church from within. Jesus spoke of two false teachings that had infiltrated the church in Pergamum.

He said that some of their group had embraced the teaching of Balaam. In the next sentence he also said that they had some who had bought into the teaching of the Nicolaitans. Both groups were using false teaching to justify engaging in immorality and idolatry. The grammatical structure of the text actually ties the two together.

Balaam was a pagan seer at the time of Israel's exodus. Balak was the king of Moab, one of the territories the Israelites were about to conquer, (see *Numbers*, chapters twenty-two through twenty-four). Balak went to Balaam and paid him to curse the Israelites. Balaam proceeded to speak five prophecies of blessing about the Israelites. When Balak chastised him for proclaiming blessings rather than curses Balaam told him that he could not curse those who God had blessed. But Balaam wanted the money. He gave Balak a strategy to get the Israelites to compromise so that God himself would judge them.

In *Numbers*, chapter twenty-five, we are told that Moabite women were sent into the camp of the Israelites to seduce the Jewish men to commit immorality and engage in idolatry. In response, God unleashed a plague that killed twenty-four thousand Jews. In the thirty-first chapter of *Numbers*, we are told that this was the advice Balaam gave to Balak. Balaam didn't disguise the sin with theological maneuvering, but the Nicolaitans did.

In his letter to the church in Ephesus, Jesus commended the Ephesians for hating the practices of the Nicolaitans, (Rev. 2:6). Scholars believe this group was teaching that grace made immorality and idolatry irrelevant. Jesus didn't agree. He hated what they taught and the destructive outcome it produced. This false teaching had infiltrated the church in Pergamum.

By the time Jesus confronted and critiqued the church, it was possible that the idolatry they were guilty of was greed. Paul had already drawn this analogy in his letters that were written before *Revelation*. We live in a time when most of us are not tempted to worship actual physical idols. But when we make the acquisition of wealth too important, we engage in the idolatry of greed. We live in a time when immorality and greed are part of our cultural *zeitgeist*. This makes the correction Jesus addressed to the church in Pergamum all the more relevant for our own times.

Repent!

The solution to the problems at Pergamum elicited the shortest message of correction contained in any of the seven letters. Jesus simply commanded, "Repent!" Let me paraphrase: "Stop it!" The church needed to turn from its moral and religious compromise and get back to living faithfully in conformity to the teaching of the Bible in these areas. The leadership of the church needed to intervene and stop both the teaching and the practices of the Nicolaitans.

Jesus reinforced his correction with a warning. If the church did not repent, and did not stop engaging in immorality and idolatry, Jesus was going to use the two-edged sword and administer judgment. We are not told the specifics of what this judgment would entail, but just the warning should have been enough to shake up the believers in Pergamum and get them to respond. As even more incentive, Christ made two great promises to those who would.

Bread and Stones

To him who overcomes, I will give some of the hidden manna, (Rev. 2:17).

Jesus made a promise about "hidden manna". In *Exodus*, chapter sixteen, we read about what happened when the Jews ran out of food early in their exodus from Egypt. Moses prayed and God provided. Every morning when they awoke, a thin, wafer-like substance would be on the ground. It was a food source that would sustain them for nearly forty years.

The Israelites were instructed to take only what they needed for one day. If they took more, it rotted. On the day before the Sabbath they were instructed to take twice what they needed so that they would not break the Sabbath by working. This time, the food lasted for two days without rotting.

The Israelites wanted to know what they were eating. They asked Moses, "What is it?" In the Hebrew language, that question was *"Man hu?"* Moses replied that it was *"Man ha."* We could paraphrase the answer as, "It is what it is." The food became known as "manna".

When the Jews built the Tabernacle, and later the Temple, three items were placed inside the Ark of the Covenant, which sat in the Holy of Holies. The three items were 1) a set of the tablets of the Ten Commandments, 2) Aaron's rod that had miraculously budded to identify him as God's chosen leader, and 3) a jar of manna.

In 587 BC, the Babylonian army destroyed the city of Jerusalem and tore down the Temple of Solomon. Tradition says that prior to the Temple being destroyed, Jeremiah went into the Holy of Holies and took the jar of manna out of the Ark of the Covenant. Fleeing from the Babylonians, Jeremiah supposedly hid the jar of manna in a cleft of a rock on Mt. Sinai. The Jews believed that when the

Messiah came, he would bring with him the jar of hidden manna. When Jesus promised that he would give those who responded to his correction some of the hidden manna, he was saying that he was the Messiah and that they would enjoy God's provision in the coming Messianic Age.

I will also give him a white stone with a new name written on it, (Rev. 2:17).

Jesus also promised that those who resisted compromise would receive a white stone with a new name written on it. There are several possibilities of what the symbol of the white stone could represent. In the ancient judicial system, a jury would vote by casting either a white stone for innocent, or a black stone for guilty. Our concept of being blackballed had its origin in this system.

In this case, the white stone would be a reference to the application of Christ's atonement to the believer's life, and the promise of an "innocent" verdict in judgment. But it is more probable that since the white stone has a new name written on it that this is a symbol of Jesus conferring special rights and privileges on the one who wins the battle against evil.

In the ancient games, winners were often given white stones to go along with their laurel wreaths. The stone guaranteed free admission to any of the games. But if you happened to be a gladiator, and one that reached the age of retirement (few did), a white stone with the words "Proven beyond a doubt" on it guaranteed that all your material needs would be met for the rest of your life.

Forgiveness, special rights and privileges, abundant provision and honor. The rewards for overcoming the temptations of compromise are far greater than any benefit gained by giving in to the temptation.

Whoever has ears, let them hear what the Spirit says to the churches!

34

CHAPTER SIX: *Letters to the churches, pt. 4*

To the angel of the church in Thyatira write: (Rev. 2:18).

Thyatira was a small, agricultural town located about forty miles southeast of Pergamum. It was not a prominent city in Asia Minor. The town's one "claim to fame" was a purple dye it produced that was used to make purple cloth. This cloth was famous throughout the Roman world. The first person to believe in Jesus in Europe was a woman named Lydia from this city who sold this cloth in the Macedonian city of Philippi, (Acts 16:14).

To a small church in this relatively obscure city, Christ addressed his longest message of all the letters to the seven churches. It would seem logical to assume that Christ singled out this particular church because of a serious problem that was taking place within the church. It was a problem all the churches were potentially facing.

Jesus began this letter by identifying himself as "the Son of God, whose eyes are like blazing fire, and whose feet are like burnished bronze," (Revelation 2:18). This is the first time the words "Son of God" appear in the book of *Revelation*. When John first received the vision of Christ, he said, "I saw one like a Son of Man." That phrase was borrowed from the book of *Daniel* and identified Jesus as the Messiah.

In this letter to the church in Thyatira, Jesus emphasized his authority. Instead of pointing to his messianic role, he reminded them he was the Son of God! The message Jesus sent to this church was tough. Christ wanted to make it perfectly clear that his authority to speak this kind of tough message rested upon the fact that he was God.

Because he is the Son of God, he has eyes that are "like blazing fire." Imagine being the object of the penetrating gaze of Jesus Christ. When he looks at us he sees into our lives and immediately discerns what is going on. He knows when we are on track with him and when something is wrong. In conjunction with His blazing eyes, Christ reminded the church that he had "feet like burnished bronze."

The word that is translated "bronze" here, and in chapter one, is not used anywhere else in the New Testament. Many scholars believe this particular metal was an alloy. Two metals were combined to make this "burnished bronze". We think the two metals were gold and bronze.

The metal would have had the appearance of a very pure and brilliant bronze. This would explain why John commented that the "bronze" looked like it had been heated to glowing in a furnace. Christ's burnished bronze feet are a symbol of divine judgment. One day, these are the feet that will trample the "winepress of God's wrath". Jesus Christ, with His eyes blazing like fire, knew the condition of the church in Thyatira, discerned the problems within the church, and with his feet of burnished bronze warned the church of their need to make some changes.

Good Things in Thyatira

There were some good things happening in this church. Jesus said, "I know your deeds, your love and faith, your service and perseverance, and that you are now doing more than you did at first," (Rev. 2:19). At first appearance, the men and women that made up the church in Thyatira seemed to be doing pretty well.

This was a church that was demonstrating the reality of Christ in their lives. It was a church that was involved in doing good things. Throughout the history of the Church, many beautiful things have happened as people have come into relationship with Jesus Christ.

At the time of the New Testament, orphans were often abandoned and left to die. Widows sometimes had to beg on the streets and at times died from exposure and starvation. There was very little concern for the poor. When people came into a vital relationship with Christ, they began to be concerned about these things.

It was the Church (with a capital "C") that started the first orphanages. It was the Church that began to care for widows. It was the Church that sought to meet the needs of the poor. The Church was involved in bringing Christ's righteousness and justice into society and initiated action that demonstrated Christ's love for the world.

Jesus went on to say, "I know your love." The word that is used here is the Greek word *agape*. In older translations of the Bible, *agape* was translated "charity." This translation of the word reflects that this kind of love involves self-sacrificial giving to meet people's needs.

This was a group of people who were involved in good works that were characterized by love. They were seeking to meet one

36

another's needs. There were loving relationships within their fellowship.

Christ continued the letter by saying, "I know your faith." Faith is a trusting reliance upon, and personal commitment to, Jesus Christ. Jesus said the church in Thyatira had faith. Christ also commended them for their serving. The word translated "service" is the Greek word *diakonia*. In secular Greek, the word described the servant who was assigned the task of waiting on tables. It was the word chosen by the early church to identify those designated to serve the more physical needs of the church body. They were called deacons (from the word *diakonia*) and deaconesses.

In the book of *Acts*, we see how those who were to fill this role needed to possess two essential qualifications. They needed to be people who were (1) full of the Holy Spirit, and (2) filled with wisdom. It takes a special grace in our lives to be a servant and to assume a serving role.

Thyatira was a church about which Christ could say, "I know your deeds, I know your love, I know your faith, I know your service, and I know your patient endurance," (Rev. 2:19). There were many pressures put on this church, and yet they endured those pressures and remained faithful to Christ.

Christ summarized his commendation by saying, "I know your last works are greater than your first." Outwardly, everything looked good. But inwardly, there were serious spiritual problems.

Jezebel and Thyatira

Nevertheless, I have this against you: You tolerate that woman Jezebel, who calls herself a prophet, (Rev. 2:20).

The problems at Thyatira again involved the issues of immorality and idolatry. The source of the problem was a woman Jesus called "Jezebel". She was apparently a self-proclaimed prophetess.

A prophet is a person through whom God speaks. "Jezebel" was probably claiming that God was giving her messages that she was to communicate to the church in Thyatira. Her messages were leading the church into moral and spiritual error.

Once again the problems in Thyatira included idolatry and immorality. Two of the greatest weapons that Satan uses in the world today are *eros* - sexual immorality, and *mammon*--

37

materialism. We tend to think of satanic activity as primarily having to do with the supernatural and occult. In reality, the greatest weapons leveled against us are the daily temptations we all face.

In all probability, the name "Jezebel" was used symbolically in this message. The original Jezebel was the wife of King Ahab of Israel. Their story can be found in the book of *I Kings*. Ahab was one of the worst kings of Israel's Northern Kingdom.

Ahab led the Northern Kingdom into the worship of Baal. Ahab began to worship Baal as a result of his marriage to a pagan woman by the name of Jezebel. Jezebel seduced Ahab - both physically and spiritually. The two primary components of Baal worship were immorality and idolatry. One reason why Baal worship was so popular was that it gave a religious stamp of approval to sexual immorality.

Jezebel started a campaign to rid the nation of Israel of the prophets of the Lord. She established her own priests and prophets who served Baal. Because of this she became a symbol to the Jewish world of spiritual corruption and false religion.

Jesus used this symbol of Jezebel to expose this woman false teacher in the church at Thyatira who, through her teaching, was drawing people in the church into immorality and idolatry.

It is possible that when Christ spoke of immorality and idolatry, he was using those concepts in symbolic terms. Any time the nation of Israel departed from the true worship of *YHWH* and began to get involved in the worship of false gods, God accused them of spiritual adultery. The classic Old Testament example is found in the book of *Hosea*. God made Hosea marry a woman who would be unfaithful to him as an object lesson of how God felt about Israel's spiritual unfaithfulness.

The church at Thyatira might have been tolerating a message that Jesus viewed as spiritual adultery. Perhaps the teaching involved something like this: "Jezebel" was receiving "prophecies." The "prophecies" that she was receiving and teaching could have implied that God's grace would allow the believer to say, "Caesar is Lord" and to burn that pinch of incense.

If you are saved by grace, what difference does it make? Go ahead and join the trade guilds and sacrifice to the idol of the trade guilds; it is irrelevant because you are saved by grace. Go ahead and eat meat sacrificed to idols and take part in the pagan practices. Through such teaching, which is a distorted form of grace, the believers in Thyatira might have been led into both physical and spiritual immorality and idolatry.

Freedom in Christ is freedom to serve God, not freedom to do anything you want to do. To say that since you are saved by grace, and consequently it is permissible to do these things, is to distort grace.

As a result of "Jezebel's" teaching, Jesus said that he was going to cast her into a "bed of affliction," (Rev. 2:22). What a contrast! On one hand, "Jezebel's" teaching leads to the bed of immorality; but Christ says that if you allow yourself to sleep in the bed of immorality, the result is that you will sleep in the bed of affliction!

Those who Jesus said "commit adultery with her" were probably those who were teaching the same false doctrine. Her "children" would be those who accepted her teaching and acted accordingly. Jesus said that he would judge those actions severely.

In order to get their house in order, the church in Thyatira was given instructions concerning what they needed to do. The most obvious, and implied, action they needed to take was to stop tolerating this false teacher and her teaching.

Jesus specifically addressed his instructions to those who had not yet been swayed by "Jezebel". He referred to her teaching as "Satan's so-called deep secrets". My educated guess is that this prophetess was claiming the things she was teaching were "the deeper secrets of God". She was probably teaching that if you understood the deeper things of God, you would understand that what she was teaching was true. It is a way of circular reasoning that is hard to logically refute. That is why you will find it in almost every cult.

Jesus turned her theology around by revealing that her so-called "deep secrets of God" were really the deep secrets of Satan! They came from the Evil spirit, not the Holy Spirit.

A Word of Encouragement

Now I say to the rest of you in Thyatira…hold on to what you have until I come, (Rev. 2:24-25).

To those that still remained faithful to Christ, and did not allow themselves to be carried away by whatever this strange teaching was, Christ said, "Hold on to what you have until I come," (Rev. 2:25). Jesus went on to promise, "To him who overcomes and does my will to the end, I will give authority over the nations," (Rev. 2:26).

The overcomer at Thyatira would be the man or woman who avoided apostasy. They would have quit tolerating Jezebel or her heresy. They would take a stand for the truth. To such men and women, Jesus Christ made two terrific promises.

Christ quoted from a Messianic psalm of David and promised the overcomer authority over the nations, (Ps. 2:9). Not only will the overcomer survive the end of the world, he or she will actually rule and reign with Christ in the age to come.

Finally, Jesus promised those who heeded his correction that he would give them the morning star. In Revelation 22:16 Christ declares, "I am the morning star." The greatest reward the faithful believer looks forward to is Christ, himself. We will know him in all his glory, fullness and power, and enjoy fellowship with him... forever!

Whoever has ears, let them hear what the Spirit says to the churches!

CHAPTER SEVEN: *Letters to the churches, pt.5*

"To the angel of the church in Sardis write: (Rev. 3:1).

The First Century Church

It is not unusual to hear people who criticize the church today say something like, "We've got to get back to the first-century church." I always wonder which one they want "to get back to." The church in the first century faced the same problems that we face in the church today. That is why the letters in these two chapters of *Revelation* are so relevant.

Jesus Christ does not want us to be the first-century church. He wants us to be the twentieth-first century church, faithful to Him in the society of our day. He does not want us looking backwards; he wants us looking upwards. If we seek to be Christ's people in the midst of our culture, we are going to face many of the challenges and problems that the churches of the first-century faced.

D.O.A.

I know your deeds; you have a reputation of being alive, but you are dead, (Rev. 3:1).

The fifth of the seven letters in *Revelation* was addressed to the church in the city of Sardis. Sardis was an extremely wealthy city. The people who lived there were notorious for their luxurious and loose way of living. The church in Sardis was not facing persecution; not experiencing hostility from the Jews; and not being troubled by heretical teaching. None of the threats the other churches faced were problems in Sardis. Yet it was a church that Christ said was "dead."

Sardis was a city that was wealthy but degenerate. The city's citizens were known for being apathetic, soft and lazy. The church, in this atmosphere, had lost its vitality. It had become conformed to the world. To be conformed to the world means that we allow ourselves to be molded by the world around us, rather than be transformed by the power of the Spirit within us.

Jesus identified himself to this church as "him who holds the seven spirits of God and the seven stars." In chapter one we were introduced to the phrase, "the seven spirits of God". The phrase could be translated "the seven-fold Spirit of God." This was a symbolic way of speaking about the Holy Spirit. This designation of the Holy Spirit is based on the prophecy of *Isaiah*, (Isaiah 11:2). There the Messiah is spoken of as one on whom the Spirit of the Lord comes to rest.

The Spirit of the Lord is described as "the spirit of the Lord, the spirit of wisdom, understanding, counsel, power, knowledge and fear of the Lord." Seven characteristics are attributed to the Holy Spirit. The phrase "the seven Spirits of God" or "the seven-fold Spirit of God" would refer to the Holy Spirit in all of his fullness and vitality. Christ said he was the one "who holds the seven spirits."

Jesus also described himself to this church as the one who "holds the seven stars". In the first chapter of *Revelation* we saw that Jesus explained the meaning of the seven stars in his hand. He said the seven stars were the "angels" or "messengers" of the seven churches."

If the seven stars represent the people who are responsible for the spiritual oversight of the churches, then much of the responsibility for the spiritual condition of the churches rests with them. Here is a church that was spiritually dead; it was a church that desperately needed the life that only the Holy Spirit could give to revitalize it.

If the church is spiritually dead and has become apathetic and lethargic, it is likely that the spiritual leaders of the church have either not confronted the people about their condition, or have drifted into the same apathy as the church they lead. To speak into that situation, Christ identified himself as the one who has control over the Spirit, and the one who holds absolute authority over the leaders of the church.

No praise for Sardis

If you look carefully at the letter to the church at Sardis, you will see that there is no commendation. This is one of two churches about which Christ has nothing good to say. Ephesus, Pergamum and Thyatira had problems, but at least in the midst of their problems there was some positive spiritual reality. In the New Testament epistles, most of us would probably characterize the church at Corinth as the church with more problems than any of the other churches. Yet, Paul commended them. Even though there were problems, they had some positive spiritual life.

On the other hand, when Paul wrote the letter to the churches of Galatia, he had nothing good to say to them. From our outward perspective, the church at Galatia might have seemed more on target than the church at Corinth. But, from Paul's perspective, their drift into legalism had produced spiritual death.

Jesus seems more concerned with the reality of the spiritual life within a church than he is with the fact that the church has problems. He can deal with the problems, but when the church is dead, he can't do anything.

Note the contrast: a church like Smyrna that was facing persecution, poverty, and problems pressing in all about them, received no criticism. On the other hand, a church like Sardis, which found itself in extremely easy circumstances: no persecution, no poverty, and no pressures, received no commendation.

There was, however, a bit of light in the darkness. Christ was able to say, "Yet you have a few people in Sardis who have not soiled their clothes," (Rev. 3:4). There is an interesting progression in the letters to these churches. Up until now, the individual churches have been relatively on target, as a whole. But within the church there had been some kind of faction or small group that Christ had to confront. Now, the situation was reversed. The church as a whole was dead, but there was a small remnant within the church that was still living in obedience to Jesus Christ.

What's wrong in Sardis

Jesus has John write to the leader of the church, "I know your deeds; you have a reputation of being alive, but you are dead," (Rev. 3:1). The primary critique Christ addressed to this church concerned spiritual life and death. When Christ talked about their reputation of being alive, he used a word that in the Greek language had special significance. The root of the word was the Greek word *zoe*.

When this word is used in the Bible it refers to spiritual life. It is a word that John used frequently when he wrote the *Gospel of John*. When John was writing about physical life, he used the Greek word *psuche*. When he wrote about the uncreated life, that only God can gives us, he used the Greek word *zoe*.

This is the life that man was originally created to possess and that made him capable of living in a relationship with God. It is a product of the Holy Spirit being present within a life. When God created Adam, he created him with both physical life and spiritual life, (Gen.2:7). He also warned Adam that if he ate from

43

the forbidden tree of the knowledge of good and evil, he would die, (Gen. 2:17). In *Genesis*, chapter three, we have the account of both Adam and Eve doing what God told them not to do. They didn't die physically. At least not immediately. But immediately something else happened. Adam hid from God. His relationship with God had been broken. He began to be afraid of God. Why? There was a break in his spiritual relationship, because Adam had died spiritually; he lost his *zoe* life. This was what God had warned him would happen. Theologians refer to the incident as "the fall of humanity". From that point forward, men and women were born physically alive, but spiritually dead.

The consistent teaching of Jesus throughout his ministry was that he came to bring life. Whenever he made a statement about this, he used the word *zoe*, or its Aramaic equivalent that was then translated into Greek as *zoe*. The gospel that has the most references to *zoe* is the one written by John. Only John records the encounter Jesus had with Nicodemus where Jesus used the expression "born again", (John 3:3,8). Jesus taught Nicodemus that unless a person has a spiritual birth, they will never see the Kingdom of heaven. It is all about life. It is all about *zoe*.

When Jesus said, "I am the way, the truth and the life," He used this word, *zoe*. In his first epistle, John wrote, "God has given us eternal life (*zoe*). This life (*zoe*) is in his son. He who has the Son has the life (*zoe*). He who does not have the Son of God does not have life (*zoe*)," (I John 5:11-12). It is black and white. Either Christ is living in your life, and you have *zoe*, spiritual life; or Christ is outside your life, and you are spiritually dead.

The church at Sardis had a reputation for being alive. In other words, people could look externally and see their church gathering together. Every Sunday morning they would meet. They sang hymns and read the letters of the Apostles and the Gospels. Externally, everything looked like they were alive. But Jesus said, "You're dead." There was no spiritual life present. There was no spiritual reality. Sardis was structurally and confessionally a church, but they had drifted from their relationship with the living Christ. The life and vitality of the Holy Spirit working in the church was absent.

Christ continued his critique by having John write, "I have not found your deeds complete in the sight of my God," (Rev. 3:2). This was a church that had not achieved the full extent of God's will.

This was a church where Christ was not Lord. They had settled for religion and missed life-giving relationship. In all probability, the first generation of believers in Sardis had a vital relationship with Jesus. The second generation did not.

Although not apocalyptic, John Bunyan's *Pilgrims Progress* also communicated truth in symbolic form. Bunyan's work was allegorical rather than apocalyptic, but both attempt to accomplish the same goal. If the church in Sardis were a character in the book, it would be as if they had come to Vanity Fair and said, "Well, I've come quite a way on my journey, and Vanity Fair looks like a nice place to settle down and live. Maybe some people should press on to the Celestial City, but I think I'll make my home here." Such was the condition of the church in Sardis.

Fixing the problems

Wake up! Strengthen what remains and is about to die, (Rev. 3:2).

Christ gave the church five directives needed to correct their situation. The first directive was, "Wake up!" They were not conscious of their condition. The first step in solving any problem is the recognition that a problem exists. Every once in a while, Christ has to "hit us over the head with a two-by-four" to get our attention and show us the problem. That is what He does here.

Christ continued, "Strengthen what remains and is about to die." I believe the Bible teaches that when Jesus comes into our lives, we can never lose Him. Theologians call this belief "eternal security". Not all would agree with me. Here, Christ recognized that this church had a little spark of life remaining. He tells them to get that spark going, to fan it into flame.

Jesus went on to have John write, "Remember what you have received and what you've heard," (Rev. 3:3). These men and women had all of the information they needed. Their problem was that they had forgotten it, and thus ceased to respond to it. God gives us biblical truth to do more than increase our intelligence. The Word of God is given to us that we might respond in obedience to it. Here, Christ had to call the church to remember what they had heard and then obey it.

The fourth directive Jesus gave was, "Repent!" Recognizing the poverty of their spiritual experience, Christ commanded them to change the futile way of life they were leading. They needed

45

to stop heading in one direction and make a hundred and eighty degree turn. Repentance would get them heading back toward Jesus.

The fifth directive was actually a warning. "If you do not wake up, I will come like a thief, and you will not know at what time I will come you," (Rev. 3:3). In John's first epistle he wrote, "And now, dear children, continue in him, so that when he appears we may be confident and unashamed before him at his coming," (I John 2:20). True believers have nothing to fear when Jesus Christ returns, because they belong to Him. But it is possible for a believer to have areas of his or her life that would cause them shame if Christ came today. Christ warned the church in Sardis in order to help them avoid that embarrassment.

In his challenge to this church, Jesus had John write, "Yet you have a few people in Sardis who have not soiled their clothes. They will walk with me, dressed in white, for they are worthy," (Rev. 3:4). The phrase "soiled clothes" is a reference to acts of unrighteousness. There is a good possibility that along with everything else that was happening in Sardis, many of the believers were allowing themselves to indulge in the sinful activities of the city.

The primary worship in Sardis was of the goddess Sybil, the "mother goddess". This worship involved some depraved types of behavior. "Soiled clothes" would paint a picture of the believer who allowed himself to be involved in these acts of unrighteousness.

But the challenge of Jesus was directed toward those who had not compromised. To these men and women Jesus made a promise:

They will walk with me, dressed in white, for they are worthy. He who overcomes will, like them, be dressed in white. I will never erase his name from the Book of Life, but will acknowledge his name before my Father and his angels," (Rev. 3:4).

To be dressed in white is a rich symbol throughout *Revelation*. In chapter six, the martyred believers, seen as souls under the altar in heaven, are given white clothing. In chapter seven, the great multitude is dressed in white. In chapter nineteen, those present at the wedding feast of the Lamb are dressed in white. Also in chapter nineteen, the armies of heaven are dressed in white as they return with Jesus at the Second Coming.

To be dressed in white is a symbol of being clothed with the righteousness of Christ. To walk with Jesus means that the one who obeys his correction will experience and enjoy an intimate relationship with the Lord. This is a promise of the relationship we will enjoy with God in the age to come.

The final promise Christ made to those who would respond to his correction was that he would never erase their names from the *Book of Life*. The *Book of Life* contains the names of all those who have made a personal commitment to Jesus Christ and received new life through spiritual birth. In chapter twenty of *Revelation,* another reference is made to the *Book of Life*. There, we see that "If anyone's name was not found written in the Book of Life, he was thrown into the lake of fire," (Rev 20:15).

A person's eternal destiny depends upon whether or not their name is written in this "book". There are times when the Bible indicates that when we come to faith in Christ our name is written in the *Book of Life*. At other times it appears as if everyone's name is written in it from before the foundation of the world, and it is only when a person rejects or neglects Jesus Christ through their entire life that his or her name is erased from the *Book of Life*.

This can be viewed as two sides of the same coin. God desires everyone to come to Christ, and He gives people that opportunity. When we come to Christ and make that commitment, it is as if permanent ink is added to our name in the "book". The most important issue that could ever be settled in our lives is whether or not we have made such a commitment.

In the church in Sardis, where there was a profession of Christianity without a possession of Jesus Christ, Christ demanded a personal commitment. When the Day of Judgment comes, it won't make any difference whether you were a deacon, an elder, a church member, or even a pastor. If you have never made a personal commitment to Jesus Christ your name will not be found in this book.

Whoever has an ear, let him hear what the Spirit says to the churches.

CHAPTER EIGHT: *Letters to the churches, pt. 6*

To the angel of the church in Philadelphia write: (Rev. 3:7).

The city of brotherly love

The sixth church Jesus picked to receive one of the seven letters was in the city of Philadelphia. The name of the city comes from one of the Greek words for love. That word is combined with the Greek word for brother. When you put it together, the name of the city meant brotherly love.

The city of Philadelphia had been built about 180 years before the birth of Christ on the borders of an area that had been untouched by Greek civilization and culture. In 133 BC it was taken over by the Roman Empire and became part of the newly formed province of Asia.

The city was a "missionary" city which had been built for the purpose of disseminating Greek culture and language into areas that were not yet "civilized." To the Greeks and Romans, anyone who did not share their culture was "uncivilized." It was a city Caesar had given an "open door" for the spread of Greek and Roman ideas in "the land beyond."

Getting it right

Jesus' message to the church in Philadelphia contained good news for a change! Most of the seven churches had serious problems. Ephesus was a church that had left its first love; Pergamum was a church that had compromised; Thyatira tolerated apostasy; Sardis was a church that was spiritually dead. Indeed, the only bright spot so far was the church at Smyrna, and that was a church in the midst of intense persecution and abject poverty.

The church in Philadelphia was not experiencing the level of difficulty the church in Smyrna was. It was simply a church that was being faithful and obedient. This church was one of two churches for which Christ had the greatest commendation.

These are words of him who is holy and true, who holds the key of David. What he opens, no one can shut; and what he shuts, no one can open," (Rev 3:7).

Jesus addressed himself to this church as "him who is holy

and true." This identification could be translated as "the Holy One and the True One". The phrase "the Holy One" comes from the prophecy of *Isaiah*. Isaiah repeatedly called God the "Holy One of Israel". In *Isaiah,* chapter 40, verse 25, God says, "To whom will you compare me? Or who is my equal?" says the Holy One." In *Isaiah* chapter 43, verse 15, God says, "I am the Lord, your Holy One. Israel's Creator, your King." This was a title of God that highlighted his holy character. Now Jesus Christ told John to write: "I am the Holy One."

Jesus went on to say that he was "the True One." There are two Greek words translated "true." One is the word *alethes* that means true, as distinguished from that which is false. The other Greek word, *alethinos*, means true in the sense of that which is real, as opposed to that which is unreal. When Christ said, "I am the True One," he used this second word. He was communicating to the church in Philadelphia that he was real and that all that is real had its source in him.

This title also echoes the claims of Jesus recorded by John in his gospel. The night before he went to the cross he shared a final meal with his disciples. It was during that meal that he told the disciples, "I am the Way, and the Truth, and the Life," (John 14:6). Christ revealed Himself to the church in Philadelphia in this way because this was a church that was rooted and grounded in the truth.

Christ also had John write that he was "the one who holds the key of David." A key in the Bible is a symbol of authority. A key is that which can give access or block access. When a person uses a key, he either opens a door to let someone in or he locks a door to keep someone out.

The specific statement that Christ made here again comes from the book of *Isaiah.* At the time Isaiah was writing a man named Shebna was the palace administrator of King Hezekiah. Isaiah's prophecy revealed that God was going to remove Shebna from that position of authority and replace him with a man named Eliakim.

The *Isaiah* text says, "He (Eliakim) will be a father to those who live in Jerusalem and to the house of Judah. I will place on his shoulders the key to the house of David; what he opens, no one can shut, and what he shuts, no one can open," (Is. 22:22).

The position that Eliakim was to assume was that of the palace steward. This was the person who had the authority to let people into the presence of the king for an audience, or to keep people out of the presence of the king. He was also the one who held the key to the treasury in the king's palace.

II Samuel, chapter 7, contains a promise God made to David about an everlasting kingdom that was going to be given to his descendants. There is a multiple fulfillment of this prophecy. The initial fulfillment took place during the reign of David's son, Solomon. From the time of Solomon, till the destruction of Jerusalem by the Babylonians, all the kings of the Southern Kingdom of Judah came from the line of David.

The ultimate fulfillment of the promise involved the establishment of an everlasting kingdom that would come through the house of David. That is why the genealogies of Jesus trace his lineage back to David; Jesus fulfills this promise. He is the messianic king who will reign forever over the Kingdom of God.

The key to the house of David represents the absolute authority over the age to come that belongs to Jesus Christ. He is the one who opens the door to the kingdom; he is the one who shuts the door. "What he opens, no one can shut; what he shuts, no one can open." He has absolute authority to let someone into the messianic kingdom; He has authority to shut someone out.

Christ began this letter to the faithful men and women of Philadelphia by telling them that he was using the key of David to place before them an open door that no one could shut. He was guaranteeing their entrance into his messianic kingdom, and encouraging their work of spreading the good news to those who lived in the spiritual "land beyond".

The things that please

I know your deeds, (Rev. 3:8).

There are four characteristics of the church in Philadelphia that Christ commended. If we want to be people who please Christ, both individually and corporately, these four characteristics must be operative in our lives and in our churches. The open door that Christ promised this church was a direct consequence of their possession of these four characteristics.

Christ began his commendation by saying, "I know your deeds," (Rev. 3:8). He used this same phrase in five of the seven letters to the churches. It introduced either what was pleasing to

Christ about the church, or what needed change. In the case of the church in Philadelphia, it was all good.

Jesus said, "I know that you have a little power," (Rev. 3:8). This statement is not a put-down. Jesus Christ was making a positive statement about the presence of spiritual reality in this church. The word translated "power" is the Greek word *dunamis*. It refers to the power of the Holy Spirit.

The Holy Spirit was present and at work in this church. This stands in stark contrast to what we saw in the church in Sardis. Sardis was dead. Why was it dead? No life. What is the source of life? The Holy Spirit. The church at Philadelphia was a church that had the life and power of the Holy Spirit operating in their midst.

Jesus did not say that they were a spiritual superpower. (I'm not sure such a thing really exists.) He simply said, "You have a little power." But, a little *dunamis* goes a long way--because it's resurrection power. This was a church where there was life, vitality, spiritual reality, and power.

Jesus also commended the church in Philadelphia because they had "kept my word." The word "to keep" is the Greek word *tereo*, which means to obey. The root idea of the word is "to protect or to guard." Philadelphia was a church that was living in obedience to Christ's word. Consistently, Jesus Christ made obedience to His Word the measure of a man or woman's love for Him.

The third quality for which Christ commended this church was their faithfulness. He said, "You have not denied my name." This word "deny" can mean several things. It can mean to disown, to renounce, or to repudiate. There are two ways that a person could deny Christ's name.

The most obvious was to renounce Jesus when confronted by the Roman government. This was the consistent problem that all these churches were facing. The second way a church or individual believer could deny Jesus was to repudiate his name by their lifestyle.

In *Titus*, chapter one, verse sixteen, the Apostle Paul makes a challenging statement. He writes, "They claim to know God, but by their actions they deny him." The same word is used in this verse that is translated "deny" in *Revelation*. Philadelphia was a church that had not denied Christ's name. Overtly, they had not renounced His name, and by their lifestyle, they had not repudiated His name.

The fourth quality that Christ commended was their perseverance. He said, "You have kept my command to endure patiently." The word used here speaks of a conquering endurance. It means to bear up courageously under suffering, affliction, and persecution. When times got tough, the church in Philadelphia patiently endured; they persevered.

What is it that Christ likes in a church? He likes at least four things. He likes to see some power--the reality of the Holy Spirit at work in a group of men and women that love Jesus. He likes obedience--people who are willing to live by the principles of His Word. He likes faithfulness--people who do not deny him in word or in action. Finally, he likes people who endure--who hang with him through the tough times. The church at Philadelphia was a church that possessed all of these qualities.

That was the reason why this is one of two churches to which Christ did not address any critique. Since this message contains no critique, it contains no correction. But Jesus did have some words of encouragement for the men and women of this church. In verse eleven He said, "I am coming soon; hold on to what you have so that no one will take your crown."

The word translated "to hold on" means to grasp something firmly so that it will not slip. The verb tense in the Greek expresses continual action. Christ was saying, "Firmly and tenaciously grasp on the power that you have; firmly and tenaciously continue to be an obedient church; firmly and tenaciously be faithful; firmly and tenaciously persevere." Why? Jesus said so that no one would take their crown.

The Bible teaches that God will reward faithfulness both in this life and in the life to come. It is staggering to think that our eternal destiny is contingent upon our faithfulness in this life. The opportunities that we have from day-to-day, and the choices that we make, are going to influence what God entrusts us with in eternity. Our time on earth is like a spiritual boot camp. God gives us this time to train us, test us, and give us a chance to develop faithfulness.

The Bible says that we can lose part of what God intends for us in the life to come by being unfaithful in this life. It is possible for us to make decisions opposed to the will of God. Someday, we might be eternally sorry for those decisions. God has given us the freedom to live our lives in any way we choose, but we can only live them once.

The Apostle Paul wrote, "Everybody that runs the race does not win the prize, so run the race in such a way that you win the crown," (I Cor. 9:24). That is Christ's challenge to us through this letter. We are to tenaciously hold on to the reality of the Spirit, live in obedience to the Word, remain faithful to His name, and endure the hard times.

Good things to come
Jesus Christ made a series of promises to the church in Philadelphia. The first is found in verse 9:

I will make those of the synagogue of Satan, who claim to be Jews, though they are not, but are liars--I will make them come and fall down at your feet and acknowledge that I have loved you.

Part of the messianic hope of the nation of Israel was that the hostile Gentile nations of the world would someday acknowledge that their God was the true God, and that he loved Israel. Jesus turned this around and made it a promise to the church. Christ promised that in the end, when the story is over, everyone will know that Jesus is the Messiah and that he loves the church.

The second promise is found in verse 10:

Since you have kept my command to endure patiently, I will also keep you from the hour of trial that is going to come upon the whole world to test those who live on the earth.

The events Jesus referred to in this promise are contained in the second part of *Revelation*. This period of coming history is called the Tribulation. It will be a cataclysmic time in human history that will be climaxed by the return of Jesus Christ.

The promise Jesus made to this church was that he would keep them from this hour of trial. Does "keep you from" mean that Christ will take them out of the world so that they will not go through the Tribulation? Or could it mean that he will protect them in the midst of the Tribulation? You will have to keep reading to find out!

The third promise Christ made is found in verse 12:

Him who overcomes I will make a pillar in the temple of my God.

What is the temple of God? The Bible teaches that the real

54

temple is not something made by human hands. In one sense, the entire universe is His temple. Later in *Revelation* John will write that in the New Jerusalem there will be no temple, because by his immediate presence, God makes the entire city a temple.

To be a pillar was symbolic of a place of importance or a position of authority. The faithful believer will hold such a position in the coming kingdom. It will be a position of authority and permanence in our relationship with God. Never again will the believer be in a position in which he does not experience the conscious reality of the presence of God.

The fourth promise involved a mark of ownership that Christ will place on the man or woman who possesses the qualities the church in Philadelphia embodied:

I will write on him the name of my God, and the name of the city of my God, the New Jerusalem, which is coming down out of heaven from my God, and I will also write on him my new name, (vs. 12).

The concept of writing a name on someone occurs twenty-seven times in *Revelation*. It is used with reference to both the name of God and the mark of the beast. There are at least five dimensions of this concept.

First, it is a sign of identification. Those who receive the mark of the beast will be identified with the beast. Those who have the name of God written on them will be identified with God.

Second, it is a mark of ownership. To have a name written on you meant you belonged to that person. The person who will bear the mark of the beast will belong to the beast; the person who has the name of God written on him will belong to God.

Third, it is a mark of citizenship. When Christ said, "I'll put the name of the New Jerusalem on them," he is promising citizenship in the New Jerusalem. Fourth, it is a symbol of authority. We carry the authority of the one with whose name we have been marked.

Finally, it involves the concept of blessing. In Numbers chapter 6, God says, "I will place my name on the Israelites and I will bless them." When you put all these together you see that the name of God written on the believer implies ownership, identification, citizenship, authority, and blessing.

Whoever has ears, let them hear what the Spirit says to the churches.

To the angel of the church in Laodicea write: (Rev. 3:14).

The final church to which Jesus addressed a letter was located in the city of Laodicea. Laodicea was one of the great commercial centers of the ancient world. It was the banking and financial center for the province of Asia. It was a city that had amassed great wealth.

Laodicea was also known for its clothing manufacture. There was a variety of sheep with jet-black wool that were raised in the area of Laodicea. From this wool, expensive garments were woven. Laodicea became known as a well-clothed city: a city whose garments were sold throughout the rest of Asia Minor.

Laodicea was also a medical center in the ancient world. Tradition tells us that a famous ophthalmologist lived here who had created an eye salve that was used throughout Asia. All these characteristics played into the message Jesus sent the church in this city.

The faithful and true witness

These are the words of the Amen, the faithful and true witness, the ruler of God's creation," (Rev. 3:14).

Jesus Christ identified himself to the church in Laodicea as "the Amen." "Amen" is an English transliteration of the Greek word *amen*, (the "e" sounds like a long "a"). *Amen* was a word placed at the beginning of a pronouncement to emphasize the veracity and certainty of the message of the pronouncement.

Jesus used this word repeatedly in his teaching. He would begin a statement by using the word twice. This added even more emphasis to his teaching. Where the text contains "Amen and amen!" our English Bibles translate the phrase "Truly, truly!" When Jesus used this formula he was emphasizing the absolute certainty of what he was saying. When Jesus identified himself by using this word, he was saying, "I am the one whose word is true and whose promises can be relied upon with complete confidence."

Jesus added to this the declaration, "I am the faithful and true witness." He is faithful and true as he reveals who God is, and as he validates the truth which God communicates in the Bible.

Jesus also called himself "the ruler of God's creation." The word translated out of Greek as "ruler" is the word *arche*. The *arche* in Greek philosophy was the first cause, the starting point, and the ultimate source of power and authority. The word carries the idea of priority, or preeminence. In terms of position, the *arche* was the one who held the highest rank. When Jesus Christ called himself the *arche*, he was proclaiming to this church that he holds the place of preeminent authority over the entire created universe.

Nothing good in Laodicea

I know your deeds, that you are neither cold nor hot, (Rev. 3:15).

If you look carefully, you will find no commendation from Jesus addressed to this church. This is the second church about which Christ had absolutely nothing good to say. This stands in stark contrast to his message to the church at Philadelphia. By knowing that he did not commend Laodicea, and remembering what he did commend at Philadelphia, we can determine what was not happening in the church in Laodicea.

The church in Philadelphia was commended for four qualities. Christ pointed out the spiritual reality that existed in the church, their obedience to the Word, their faithfulness, and their willingness to suffer hardship for the cause of Christ. If Christ commended the church at Philadelphia for these things, and had no commendation for the church at Laodicea, then we can assume that all four of those qualities were absent at Laodicea.

This was a church lacking spiritual vitality. Like the church in Sardis, they were spiritually dead. This was a church that was not living in obedience to the Word of God. They were not being faithful to Jesus Christ, and they lacked perseverance in the face of difficulty.

Think how horrid it would be to stand in the presence of Jesus and hear him say, "I do not have one good thing to say about you." Can you imagine Jesus telling you that you make him want to vomit? That is exactly what he said to the church in Laodicea.

The intensity of Jesus' message to this church was triggered by what at first glace might seem like a minor problem. This was a church that Jesus said was "lukewarm". He points out that they were neither hot nor cold. In context, it is not an external temperature he is speaking about. He is referring to the spiritual "temperature" of the church.

The Greek word for "hot" is *zestos*, from which we get our word "zest". The word was used to describe a person who was fervent and zealous - someone who was extremely devoted to a cause. Unfortunately, this was not the case with the church in Laodicea. They were not hot.

Jesus also said, "You are not cold." The Greek word for cold is *psuchros*. It was a word that was used figuratively to speak of stony indifference. In this case, Christ indicated that even indifference would be better than their actual "temperature". They were not hot...and they were not cold. They were just lukewarm.

There were three different kinds of water sources in the area of Asia Minor. Hierapolis was a city located six miles from Laodicea. Hierapolis was known for its natural hot springs. These hot springs were famous for their medicinal value and were considered healing waters. Their water was hot.

Another town close to Laodicea was the town of Colossae. This was the city where the church was located to which the New Testament letter *Colossians* was written. Colossae had naturally cold springs. The cold kept the water pure. On the one hand, Hierapolis had hot water that possessed healing value, and on the other hand, Colossae had ice-cold water that was pure. Laodicea did not have either.

Laodicea had its water supply piped into the city via an aqueduct. The water traveled far enough that by the time it reached Laodicea it had become lukewarm. In its lukewarm state it was so impure that if a person drank the water before it was boiled it would make them sick, causing them to vomit. Jesus evaluated the spiritual condition of this church and said that their wealth and self-sufficiency had led to a spiritual condition like the water supply into their city. Because of the lukewarm spiritual condition of the church Jesus said he was about to "spew them out." The word in the Greek that is translated "to spew" is *emesia*, from which we get our word, emetic. "Emetic" means, "that which produces nausea and causes one to vomit." By using this language Jesus was telling this church that their spiritual condition made Him so sick that he wanted to vomit.

From the early days of church history, "lukewarm" became a word that was used by the church fathers to refer to an unregenerate person professing to be a Christian. Men and women might call themselves "Christian," but if they had never had the encounter with Jesus Christ that produced spiritual life, they were just "lukewarm".

To add to the problems present in this church, it would appear that they were oblivious to their pathetic spiritual condition. Jesus said, "You say, 'I am rich, I have no need.'" The worst condition in which a spiritual person can find himself or herself is to be at a point in their spiritual life where they think they have no need. It is the height of confusion and self-deception.

Need is a good thing. It is need that forces us to depend on Jesus Christ. The man or woman who is living in a vital relationship with God is aware of how much they need his mercy and grace. When a person drifts into complacency, oblivious to their real condition, they need a spiritual reality check. This was exactly what Jesus did in this letter.

The Christians in Laodicea were rich and oblivious to their true spiritual condition. Jesus told them their true state was one of being "wretched... pitiful... poor...blind...and naked."

Remember the words Jesus sent to the church in Smyrna? He said, "I know you are poor (*ptochas*)... but you are rich (*plousios*)." To Laodicea, he says, "You say you are rich (*plousios*), but you are actually poor (*ptochas*). Their material wealth had led to spiritual poverty. There was a total reversal of conditions in these two churches.

In a city that prided itself on being a place where people came to have their eyesight restored, Jesus said the church was blind. In a city that was renown for producing fine garments, Jesus said the church was naked. In a city that was proud of their self-sufficiency, Jesus said the church was pitiful. What a contrast: materially, they had accumulated great wealth; medically they were famous for restoring eyesight; sartorially they wore the finest clothing in Asia; but spiritually, they were poor, blind, and naked.

Fixing things in Laodicea

I counsel you to buy from me gold refined in the fire, (Rev. 3:18).

The counsel and correction Jesus gave this church would lead us to wonder if they really were Christians at all. He counseled them to buy gold refined in fire. He was not speaking of physical gold. Gold is a symbol of deity. Gold refined in fire is a symbol of the indwelling presence of God that becomes ours when Christ comes to live within us.

Jesus also said, "I counsel you to buy white clothes to wear to cover your shameful nakedness." People in Laodicea desired the physical clothing made from black wool. In contrast, Jesus counsels the church to "buy" white clothes. White clothing symbolizes the righteousness of Jesus Christ. We are "naked" spiritually in the presence of God because we have no righteousness. When we receive Christ, the Bible says we become "clothed" in his righteousness.

Jesus went on to admonish them, "Buy from me salve so that you can see." Here is the city that is world famous for the eye salve that helped people see physically. Jesus played off this characteristic of the city and said that the church needed a spiritual salve from him to heal their spiritual blindness.

The salve He speaks of here is the work of the Holy Spirit, which enables us to see our true condition and our spiritual need. In Psalms 119:18, the psalmist prays, "Open my eyes so that I might behold wonderful things in your law." The church in Laodicea needed "Dr. Jesus'" spiritual eye salve.

In the midst of his counsel Jesus exclaimed, "Those whom I love, I rebuke and discipline," (Rev. 3:19). This is one of the few times when Jesus does not use the word *agape* to express his feelings for the church. Here he used the word *phileo*. This is a word that means "tender affection." For those for whom he has great affection, Jesus does two things.

First, Jesus rebukes those he loves. The word translated "rebuke" means "that which brings sin to light and demands response." Rebuke ideally leads to conviction. Conviction then leads to discipline. The word translated "discipline" is the Greek word *paideuo*, which refers to the training and education by which a child grows to maturity. Jesus' discipline is not punitive; it is corrective. He desires to deal with every area of our lives that keep us from his best.

In light of his rebuke, Jesus commanded the church in Laodicea to, "Be earnest and repent!" To "be earnest" literally means to "get hot." Christ was challenging them: "You're not hot, and you're not cold; you're just lukewarm. Get hot! Become fervent about your faith in me. Repent from your self-sufficiency and spiritual mediocrity."

Opening the door

Jesus offered this church a fantastic invitation. He said, "Here I am; I stand at the door and knock; if anyone hears my voice and opens the door I will go in and eat with him and he with me," (Rev. 3:20). This verse is often used to invite a person to begin a relationship with Jesus Christ. Some scholars would say you should not use this verse in such a way because it is written to a church. It is written to a church, but it is written to a church that appears not to have any personal relationship with Jesus.

Jesus will not force himself upon us, but he does require us to make a decision. He promised the church in Laodicea that if they would open the door (representing the door of their lives and the spiritual door of their church) and invite him to come in, he would eat with them. The word used in this passage described the evening meal. This was the main meal of the day, at which the family would sit at the table, share life together, and enjoy each other's company. This is the picture that Jesus Christ paints. When we "open the door" of our lives, and invite him to come and dwell in us, we are able to enjoy the most intimate, warm, and friendly kind of fellowship with Jesus!

To him who overcomes I will give the right to sit with me on my throne, (Rev. 3.21).

The eastern throne was often constructed like a couch. One who shared authority with the king could sit with him on the throne. Christ promised the church in Laodicea that if they would respond to his critique and correction he would share with them his authority and reign in the age to come. Like much of the message of *Revelation*, this promise is so fantastic that it should motivate us to be sure we are living in the kind of relationship with Jesus that pleases him.

Putting it all together

Although these seven letters were originally sent to seven literal churches in the Roman province of Asia, it was not long before they began to circulate among the other churches around the Roman Empire. The writings of early Christian leaders throughout the second and third centuries show that *Revelation* was used as an inspired work in the life of the churches. When the time came to make decisions about which documents would become part of the canon of the New Testament, the book of *Revelation* was included.

The early church recognized that in the messages of Jesus to these seven churches there was universal truth. If we summarize the main messages of each letter we would hear Jesus saying to us: 1) Keep me first; 2) Stay faithful; 3) Don't compromise God's truth; 4) Don't tolerate false teaching; 5) Stay spiritually alive; 6) Keep my Word; 7) Get hot!

These were the messages Jesus sent to the church in Asia. They were messages to the entire church in the first century; they are messages for the church today.

Whoever has ears, let them hear what the Spirit says to the churches.

PART TWO
The Things that are to Come

CHAPTER TEN: *The Throne in Heaven*

At once I was in the Spirit, and there before me was a throne in Heaven with someone sitting on it, (Rev. 4:2)

A Quick Trip to Heaven

As we move into the next chapters of *Revelation*, we transition to the future dimension of the book. Chapters four and five contain the interpretive key to the rest of the book. All the events contained in the rest of *Revelation* are connected to what happens when John is caught up into the presence of God.

The fourth chapter of *Revelation* begins with the words "after these things". When Jesus gave John his initial instructions to write what is now the final book of the Bible, he specified three items John was to write. He was to write what he had seen. The encounter with Jesus contained in chapter one was John's response to that part of Jesus' commission.

Jesus also told him to write "the things that are". The letters to the seven churches completed this part of the commission. Finally, Jesus told John that he was to write the things that would take place "after these things". The Greek phrase that is translated "after these things" is *meta tauta*. These are the identical words that open the fourth chapter of *Revelation*. From chapter four through chapter twenty-two *Revelation* "unveils" the future.

Notice that the location of the vision shifts in the beginning of chapter four. John was taken, "in the Spirit", into the actual presence of God. He had moved outside the time-space continuum and into the eternal realm. What he experiences in this realm is beyond John's ability to describe. Notice how often the word "like" appears in these two chapters.

These next two chapters not only contain the interpretive key to understanding the prophetic message of the Apocalypse, they also contain critical truths to help us understand life on planet Earth. If you are able to understand and embrace the truth of these two chapters, life and the future will take on new meaning and direction. If you fail to comprehend or believe what is revealed in these chapters, life will remain confusing until the end of the age actually arrives.

John tells us that as he was on Patmos he saw a door open in the heavens, and heard a voice say, "Come up here." Instantly, John tells us he entered into another dimension. Whether in the body or in some ecstatic experience in the realm of the Spirit, John found himself in heaven. The Greek word translated "heaven" is the word *ouranos*. Scientists named the eighth planet of our solar system Uranus after this Greek word we translate as "heaven". This word was used three different ways in the New Testament.

The word was used to speak of the physical heavens that surround the earth, and in which our planet moves through its orbit. When used this way the word encompasses the sky, atmosphere, and physical realm of the stars and heavenly bodies.

At other times this word was used to speak of what we call the "heavenlies". This use of the word refers to the spiritual realm of existence. It is a dimension where the activity of angels and demons occurs. It is also a realm that constantly interacts with our normal physical universe. Paul wrote, "For our struggle is not against flesh and blood, but against the rulers, against the authorities, against the powers of this dark world and against the spiritual forces of evil in the heavenly realms," (Eph. 6:12). Paul was speaking of this spiritual reality. Sometimes, this realm is referred to as the "second heavens".

The third use of this word refers to Heaven as the dwelling place of God. Since God is infinite and omnipresent when Heaven is said to be his dwelling place it is in the sense that this is a "place" where the glory and power of God finds its focal point of manifestation. This is the way the word is used here in *Revelation*.

In the Spirit, John was taken into the manifested presence of the glory of God. He saw a vision of the spiritual center of the universe. In this "place" John saw and heard things that give meaning and significance to life, and unlock the mysteries of the future.

The first thing John saw in Heaven was a throne. A throne in the ancient world was the seat of authority, power, strength, and dominion. It was a place of unique exaltation and superiority. It was a place of control from which action originated. The real message of *Revelation* (and actually of the Bible as a whole) is that there is a throne in Heaven.

The creation of the universe was not a haphazard occurrence. History is not spinning wildly out of control toward an unknown destiny. Neither are our lives. There is a throne in heaven. The universe is a purposeful creation. The cosmos is not in state of chaos. It is headed toward a predestined end. Life has meaning and purpose precisely because there is a throne in heaven.

Just as important as the existence of this throne is the fact that it is occupied. John simply said, "someone was sitting on it". This statement abolishes two of the major philosophies or worldviews held by millions of men and women in the world today. There are really only three possible worldviews that make any sense. Every philosophy of life is some variation of one of these three positions.

"Worldview One" confidently asserts that there is no throne. This position represents much of human philosophy since the fall of man, and more recently much of western thought since the time of the Enlightenment. The so-called "New Atheism" is a variation on this worldview.

Secular humanism, optimistic existentialism, and pessimistic nihilism are all expressions of this worldview. This belief system logically leads to the conclusion that history has no destiny apart from what humanity creates, and any meaning given to life is relative and a product of human scripting. The most honest conclusion of this philosophy is nihilism, which denies the existence of any meaning or purpose. There is no throne.

"Worldview Two" believes there is a throne, but it is something, not someone who occupies the throne. The something that occupies the throne is some expression of all that is. The throne is an impersonal force. From classical Hinduism, to New Age thought, to the Force of George Lucas' *Star Wars*, the throne is impersonal.

Life is circular according to this view, destined to repeat itself in a million spins of the Great Mandela. History is heading toward the next reincarnation, and all that happens is deterministically a product of karma. Meaning is what you decide it is for you. But if meaning and direction are a function of each individual's whims and fantasies, life is still meaningless. The motto of this worldview could be: "There is a throne, and we all sit on it."

"Worldview Three" is an expression of the vision John received on Patmos. There is a throne in heaven and Someone is sitting on it. People who hold this worldview believe that God exists and that he controls the ultimate destiny of humanity and the universe. This is a worldview grounded in faith in the revealed message of the Bible. History is teleological. God is God. Life has meaning and purpose. There is a throne in heaven; and it is occupied!

The theme of thrones is central to the message of *Revelation*. This concept will appear in a number of contexts throughout the book. The great question answered in Revelation is, "Which throne will prevail?" The answer to that question begins by observing the one John sees seated on this throne.

The One on the Throne

John refers to the occupant as a person, and yet his description makes no attempt at anthropomorphic detail. Rather, he describes the person in terms of flashing, brilliant light of various colors. In the Old Testament we have a record of an experience, similar to John's, that the prophet Isaiah had, (see *Isaiah*, chapter six). Isaiah was worshipping in the Temple in Jerusalem. While in the Temple, God appeared to him and spoke to him. God was seated on the throne.

John's description fits with the statement made by the Apostle Paul when he wrote to Timothy that God is the one who "dwells in unapproachable light," (I Tim. 6:16). Remember that Paul had also had a similar experience to John's but Paul had been forbidden to communicate what he saw and heard, (see II Corinthians, chapter twelve).

John used the word "like" repeatedly in his description of what he saw. He was attempting to describe the indescribable and certain comparisons and similes are as close as he could come. He described God's appearance in terms of brilliant radiating stones. The description includes three characteristics. It was first and foremost like a jasper stone. The jasper of John's day was like our diamond. It was a multi-faceted stone of incredible radiance.

The second stone he mentions is the carnelian. This was a stone that was similar to our ruby. It was a stone with a brilliant blood-red hue. There is symbolism in these colors of purity, glory, and holiness. Finally, John says a rainbow with the radiance of an emerald encircled the throne.

John was seeing a manifestation of God in all his glory. God is the one who occupies the throne. He is the sovereign ruler of heaven and earth. He is pure, holy, and radiant in his majesty. There is a throne in heaven and God occupies it. This is a major biblical truth confirmed by John's experience recorded in *Revelation*.

As John continued to describe the heavenly scene he wrote that he saw twenty-four other thrones that surrounded the throne of God. John describes those seated on them as "elders" who are dressed in white and wear golden crowns. The position of these thrones indicates that these elders share in the rule and reign of the One on the throne.

An elder in Old Testament times was a leader of the Jewish people. They were always older men who possessed the godly wisdom only age produces. Twelve of the twenty-four elders John sees possibly represent the Old Testament people of faith.

An elder in the New Testament is one who holds an office of leadership in the church. Twelve of these elders possibly represent the New Testament people of faith. The combined twenty-four are symbolic of the leadership of the people of God in Heaven. Along with these visual references John says that flashes of lightning, rumbling thunder were part of the heavenly vision.

Around the main throne, and within the circle of the twenty-four elders, John saw four living creatures. These creatures are what the Bible calls seraphim and cherubim. They are celestial beings belonging to the heavenly realm. Their appearance reflects something of the nature of the one they serve and worship.

One had the appearance of a lion; one of a calf; one had the appearance of a man; and the fourth had the appearance of an eagle. The four faces of the seraphim reflect the four dimensions of the work of Christ as portrayed in the four gospels. The lion is symbolic of Christ as portrayed in the gospel of Mathew. In Matthew, Christ is the Lion of the tribe of Judah, the Messianic King. The calf, or the ox, was a beast of burden. This image is symbolic of the portrait of Christ found in the gospel of Mark. In Mark's gospel, Jesus is the servant-King. The man is symbolic of Christ as portrayed by Luke. Luke's gospel emphasizes Jesus in his perfect humanity. The eagle is a symbol of deity. This would be consistent with the picture of Christ contained in John's gospel. John's emphasis was upon Jesus as the Son of God. Here, in the appearance of the seraphim, we see symbolically the Christ they worship.

John further describes a manifestation of the Spirit in front of the throne, (vs.5), and a sea of glass, clear as crystal before the throne. The entire scene gives new meaning to the word awesome! In light of what John sees, it is not hard to understand what he hears.

The entire heavenly scene is filled with worship. The seraphim exalt the holiness of God. Their praise also gives us a hint of what is to come in the future:

Holy, holy, holy, is the Lord God Almighty,
Who is, and was, and is to come.

71

As soon as the seraphim started to worship the elders joined in. They cast their crowns before the throne and proclaimed the worthiness of the one who sits enthroned. The casting of their crowns was an acknowledgement of their unworthiness. They knew they didn't deserve to be redeemed, or to be in Heaven. It was all a gift from God made possible by what Jesus accomplished on the cross. Their actions and worship were all a response to God's love and grace.

The throne and the future

The logical question to ask at this point is what John's vision has to do with the future. The answer: everything! The future is a product of this great fact: there is a throne in heaven with someone sitting on it. The future is controlled by the one who sits on this throne. At a time when John and the early church might have been wondering if God still cared, God wanted John to know, and to communicate to the church, he was still on the throne.

The destiny of the cosmos and the destiny of humanity depend on having a relationship with the one seated on the throne and the one who will join him in the next chapter. The most critical moment in cosmic history is about to unfold!

CHAPTER ELEVEN: *The Lamb and the Scroll*

Then I saw in the right hand of him who sat on the throne, a scroll with writing on both sides and sealed with seven seals, (Rev. 5:1).

The scroll

John tells us that he saw a scroll in the right hand of God the Father. I can't overstate the importance of this scroll. All the events of chapters six through nineteen of *Revelation* are written inside this scroll. As the scroll is opened, God's final plans and purposes will begin to unfold.

A scroll of this type had several purposes in the ancient world. A will was often contained on a scroll like this. The content of the estate was recorded inside the scroll. The scroll was then sealed with seven seals. Each seal represented a witness to the will. In order for that will to be opened and executed, those seven witnesses, or their representatives, had to be present.

In the Jewish world, deeds were often written on scrolls. The description of a piece of property was written inside the scroll. The scroll was then sealed with seven seals. The terms for opening the scroll and taking possession of the property were written on the outside of the scroll. When someone could prove they met the requirements, they could break the seals and claim the property. Notice that John said this scroll had writing on the inside and the outside.

In some Old Testament books, prophetic messages were contained on scrolls. God instructed certain prophets to eat the scroll and then speak the message contained within the scroll. Jeremiah wrote, "I found your words and ate them. And your words became a joy and delight to me, (Jeremiah 15:16). The scroll itself, and the reading of the scroll, produced the events that were written within the scroll.

This particular scroll functions in all three of these ways. It contains God's will. The final settlement of the affairs of the universe is contained within this scroll. Symbolically, this scroll could also be viewed as the title deed to Planet Earth.

In *Genesis* man was given legal authority over Earth. Earth still belonged to the Lord, in the sense of ownership, but man was given authority to rule over God's creation. In chapter three of *Genesis*, Adam and Eve chose to obey Satan rather than to obey God. When that choice was made, legal dominion over Earth was forfeited to Satan. Satan became the ruler, or "the prince of this world." On three different occasions (John 12:31; 14:30; 16:11), Jesus referred to Satan as the ruler of this world. If we do not understand this fact, we cannot understand the events that take place in the world, and we cannot understand the message of *Revelation*.

Under Jewish law, a person did not lose title to his property permanently. He forfeited title for a specific period of time. Let's imagine you owed me money and could not pay the debt. Maybe you had to forfeit your house to pay the debt. I would not own your house permanently. I would only own your house for six years. A document would be drawn up. Inside the document the piece of property you were forfeiting would be identified. On the outside of the document the conditions required for you to reclaim that property would be listed. Then the document would be sealed seven times.

At the end of the sixth year, if you could meet the requirements listed on the document, you could redeem your house. If you could not meet the requirements, your next of kin would have the option of redeeming the property, so it could be kept in the family. He would become known as a kinsman redeemer. Consider this possible scenario:

Six thousand years ago, Adam and Eve forfeited the title deed of Earth to Satan. For 6,000 years, Satan has held dominion over the world. As the 7,000th year approaches, a scroll appears in Heaven. It is the title deed to Earth. A mighty angel proclaims in a loud voice, "Who is worthy to break the seals and open the scroll?" (Rev. 5:2). He is asking, "Who meets the requirements to redeem Earth from Satan's dominion?"

John said that no one in heaven, or earth, or under the earth was found who was worthy to open the scroll. As a result, he wept, (Rev. 5:3,4). The way he describes his response could more accurately be translated as "wept hysterically". Why was it so hard to find someone who met the requirements written on the scroll?

The requirements are stiff! Because humanity was entrusted with dominion, and then forfeited the dominion, it requires a man to meet the requirements and be found worthy to open the scroll. But it needed to be a special kind of man.

Only God can redeem a human life. Along with the requirement to be a man, the only man that could open the scroll also needed

74

to be God. The one who could meet the requirements had to be both a man and God. That narrows the field! As long as no one was found who could open this scroll and reclaim the title deed, Earth would remain under the dominion of Satan. Someone had to be found who was worthy, or nothing would change. Death, pain, suffering, illness, natural and unnatural disasters would continue. No wonder John wept!

The Lion Who Is a Lamb

In the midst of his despair, John was comforted by one of the twenty-four elders that surround the throne of God. John was told, "Do not weep! See, the Lion of the tribe of Judah, the Root of David, has triumphed. He is able to open the scroll and its seven seals," (Rev. 5:5).

Who is the one who is found worthy to redeem the scroll? The elder told John, "He is the Lion of the tribe of Judah." This is a reference to the Old Testament prophecy in *Genesis* of the coming Messiah, (Gen. 49:10). The elder also said he is, "the Root of David". He fulfills the prophecy found in *Isaiah* concerning the lineage of the coming Messiah, (Is. 11:1-10).

John turned to see this Lion and instead saw a Lamb. The Lamb was standing in the middle of the throne. He shares the rule and reign over the universe with the one who sits on the throne. Of course the Lamb is Jesus Christ. He is the living Lamb who had been slain. He is the God/Man: fully God...fully man. His sacrificial death fulfilled the prophecy of John the Baptist, "Behold, the Lamb of God who takes away the sin of the world!" (Jn.1:29). Because of who Jesus Christ is, and what he has done at the cross of Calvary, he is worthy; he fulfills all of the scroll's requirements.

John watched as the Lamb took the scroll from the hand of the one who sat on the throne. When that occurred, the elders and the four creatures broke out in praise of the Lamb:

You are worthy to take the scroll and to open its seals, because you were slain, and with your blood you purchased for God persons from every tribe and language and people and nation. You have made them to be a kingdom and priests to serve our God, and they will reign on the earth, (Rev. 5:9-10).

They were then joined by innumerable angels who added to the heavenly worship:

75

Worthy is the Lamb, who was slain, to receive power and wealth and wisdom and strength and honor and glory and praise! (Rev. 5:12).

Finally all of creation joins in:

To him who sits on the throne and to the Lamb be praise and honor and glory and power, for ever and ever! (Rev. 5:13).

There is a throne in Heaven! It is occupied! The one who sits on the throne controls the destiny of the entire universe. In the center of the throne, sharing the throne, there is a Lamb who was slain and yet lives. His life was given to redeem mankind.

There is a scroll in Heaven. It contains God's perfect plans for redeeming the universe. Only the Lamb can open this scroll. Only he is worthy. The Lamb takes the scroll and prepares to open the seals. When he does, the final redemption of the created universe will begin. When we recognize the authority and power of the Lamb to accomplish such a task, we also should break forth in praise and proclaim, "Worthy is the Lamb who was slain!"

CHAPTER TWELVE: *The Scroll is Opened*

Breaking the seals

Chapters six through nineteen of *Revelation* contain a vision of a cataclysmic period of human history. It is called The Tribulation. As we move through these chapters we will see a series of divine judgments being executed upon an unbelieving world. As the Lamb opens each of the six seals on the scroll, God initiates acts of judgment upon the earth. The opening of the seventh seal introduces us to seven angels with seven trumpets. As each of these seven angels sounds his respective trumpet more intense acts of judgment are executed upon the earth. The sounding of the seventh trumpet leads to the vision of seven more angels holding seven bowls containing the final wrath of God. The outpouring of these bowls completes God's judgment of the world.

When you put this together, you can see that *Revelation* contains three sets of seven judgments. Certain numbers carry symbolic significance in the Bible. The number three is symbolic of God. The number seven is symbolic of completeness or perfection. These three sets of seven judgments represent God's perfect and complete judgment on a world that has been terribly distorted from his original intentions. These judgments represent the process whereby Earth is redeemed to its original ownership so that it might be restored to its original purposes. Even God's judgment is redemptive at heart.

The Four Horsemen of the Apocalypse

I watched as the Lamb opened the first of the seven seals...and there before me was a white horse, (Rev. 6:1.2).

The White Horse

When Jesus opened the first seal John saw a rider on a white horse. The rider wore a crown and was armed with a bow. John said this horse and its rider rode out to conquer.

There are two diametrically opposed opinions about the rider on the white horse. Some believe that the rider is Jesus Christ. In chapter nineteen of *Revelation* Jesus is pictured as a rider on a white horse wearing a crown when he returns at his second coming.

Although Jesus does wear a crown and does ride a white horse, he wields a sword. Here the rider is armed with a bow. A bow was a symbol of human military strength. In chapter nineteen, Christ wields the *rhomphaia*, the sword of divine judgment. Christ does wear a crown, but the word translated "crown" in chapter nineteen is a different word than the word that appears here in chapter six. The word for crown used here is the Greek word *stephanos*, the victor's crown discussed earlier. The crown worn in Revelation chapter nineteen is the *diadema*, the royal crown of a king. The rider in *Revelation* chapter six does not wear the royal crown and does not wield the sword of judgment. He wears the crown of conquest, and wields the bow of human military might. The white horse in both places is a symbol of victory. In chapter nineteen it represents the victory of Christ as He comes to rule over the earth. Here in chapter six, it represents the victory of human military conquest.

If the symbol of the rider on the white horse does not represent Jesus, it is possible that it represents the beginning of the activities of Antichrist. *Daniel* chapter nine describes a scenario of end-times events from Daniel's day to our own. It contains a timetable of seventy "weeks." The literal meaning of the Hebrew word *shabua*, translated "weeks," is "seven." It was a word used to speak of time periods of seven. In retrospect, we can see that the "weeks" Daniel was speaking of were periods of seven years.

The timetable was to begin with a decree to rebuild Jerusalem. That decree was issued in 445 B.C. by the Persian king, Artaxerxes, and is recorded in the Old Testament book of *Nehemiah*, (Neh. 2:1-8). According to the *Daniel* prophecy, forty-nine years, or seven "weeks" after 445 B.C., Old Testament history would come to a close. Historically, by the time the seven "weeks" were finished the walls of Jerusalem and the Temple had been rebuilt. The last book of the Old Testament was written around 396 BC.

Sixty-two "weeks", or 434 years, later would take us to approximately 30 A.D. The prophecy said that at this time the Messiah, or Anointed One, would come. Then the prophecy said the Anointed One would be "cut off" and "will have nothing."

In approximately 30 A.D., the Messiah, Jesus Christ, came. He was "cut off" at His crucifixion. After the Messiah was cut off, the prophecy said that the people of the ruler who would come (note the phrase, "the ruler who will come") would destroy Jerusalem and the Temple. From 66 to 70 A.D. the Roman army set siege to

78

Jerusalem. In 70 A.D. the Roman general Titus breached the walls of Jerusalem, annihilated the city, and destroyed the Temple. In the worlds of the prophecy, the end came "like a flood."

The above history accounts for sixty-nine of the seventy "weeks". Many scholars believe that we have been living in a prophetic gap period in the seventy "weeks" of Daniel. One seven "week" period is left to complete the vision. The prophecy first talked about "the people of the prince who is to come"; then in verse 27, the language shifts to "he", that is, the actual ruler who is to come. The ruler "who is to come" is the Antichrist. The final "week" (seven years) of Daniel's prophecy begins when Antichrist enters into a treaty with the restored nation of Israel. We will look more closely at this diabolical character when we get deeper into *Revelation.*

The Apostle Paul wrote about these same events in his second letter to the church in Thessalonica. He wrote about "the man of lawlessness," (II Thessalonians 2:3). This is another title for the Antichrist. We are told in the text that this person is being restrained, but when the restraining force is removed, the Antichrist will rise to power. When the first seal is broken, it is possible that the restraining power of God that has been holding back Antichrist and his activities is removed. When that happens, a conqueror rides forth in conquest.

Under this approach a series of political and military encounters will launch the actual tribulation period. When Antichrist rises, he initially will be viewed as a man of peace. When he enters into the alliance with Israel he will be hailed as a hero. That is one reason he is pictured riding on a white horse wearing a crown. At first glance, whom does he look like? He looks like Jesus Christ. When Antichrist begins his rise to power, he is going to look like the savior of the world.

The Red Horse

When the Lamb opened the second seal...another horse came out, a fiery red one, (Rev. 6:3-4).

When Jesus opened the second seal John saw a fiery red horse with a rider that was give a large sword. This is not the Greek *rhomphaia*, the sword of divine judgment, but rather the *machaira*, the sword of human military conquest. The rider on this horse takes peace from the world and instigates war. The events that happen when the second seal is broken show us that the tribulation period will be a time of world warfare. War sets the stage for the third horseman.

The Black Horse

When the Lamb opened the third seal... I looked and there before me was a black horse, (Rev. 6:5).

The third horseman and his black horse symbolize worldwide economic collapse. The rider on the black horse holds a pair of scales. This is a symbol that comes directly from the Old Testament. Whenever a time of economic scarcity came upon the land of Israel, they were said to have to "eat bread weighed by measure," (Lev. 26:26). The scales are a symbol of scarcity.

The severity of this scarcity can be determined by the message one of the living creatures speaks. The message is that a quart of wheat will cost a denarius. A denarius was the average day's wage for the common workingman. A quart of wheat was the bare minimum food requirement for an average family. Three quarts of barley was the equivalent of a quart of wheat.

The Tribulation will be a time when a man will have to work an entire day just to put food on the table. Normally, at the time *Revelation* was written, a denarius would buy eight to sixteen quarts of wheat. The economic situation changes so radically that what would once buy eight to sixteen quarts now will only buy one quart. Hyperinflation grips the world's economy.

The voice goes on to say, "Do not damage the oil and the wine." Oil and wine were more of a luxury than wheat and barley. Luxuries are plentiful, but necessities are scarce. This might portray a situation in which there is a worldwide economic collapse, where the normal person will struggle to have the bare necessities of life while the economic elite will scarcely be affected.

The Pale Horse

When the Lamb opened the fourth seal... I looked and there before me was a pale horse, (Rev. 6:7).

When the fourth seal was opened John saw a pale horse. He

said that the rider of this horse was Death! John says that Death was followed by Hades. These two inflict massive casualties upon the earth. Through war, famine, plague, and wild beasts one-fourth of the world's population will die.

This image has a direct link to the Old Testament. The prophet Ezekiel wrote about a time when God was going to unleash judgment on the nation of Judah for their idolatry and unfaithfulness. Ezekiel wrote:

For this is what the Sovereign Lord says. How much worse will it be when I send against Jerusalem my four dreadful judgments--sword, and famine and wild beasts and plague, (Ezekiel 14:21).

This is the exact language that is used here in *Revelation*. This judgment is directed at a specific group of people. The rider of this horse is "Death," but "Hades" is following close behind him. In the Hebrew understanding of the afterlife, the abode of the dead was called *Sheol*. The Jews during Old Testament times, and even at the time of Jesus, had a concept that the afterlife took place in a compartment somewhere inside the earth.

Inside of *Sheol* there were two divisions: Hades, and Paradise. The righteous dead went to Paradise, while the unrighteous dead went to Hades. Hades was a synonym for what we would call Hell. Jesus told a story about a poor man named Lazarus, (Luke 16:19-31). Since it would be the only parable in which Jesus used a proper name, it is possible that he was not telling a parable, but reporting an actual event.

In the story, the rich man found himself in Hades while Lazarus ended up in Paradise (sometimes called Abraham's bosom). They were able to see each other, but they were told that a great chasm separated the two, and no one was able to cross over to either side. The fact that Hades follows close behind death tells us that this judgment is targeted at the unrighteous. God's judgment is directed at those who do not have a relationship with Him.

The elephant in the room

Before we look at what happens as the rest of the seals are opened I need to address an issue that will determine how you understand the rest of *Revelation*. Where is the church during the Tribulation? Historically, there have been three primary answers to this question.
Pre-trib

In recent years, there has been a strong emphasis in certain Evangelical circles regarding the rapture of the church. The rapture is an event Paul teaches about in his first letter to the church in Thessalonica (see *I Thessalonians* 4:13-17). One generation of living believers will not experience death. While still alive they will be caught up to be with Jesus. Due in large part to a number of well-known pastors who come from a theological tradition called dispensationalism the idea of the church being taken out of the world prior to the Tribulation has enjoyed widespread popularity. This position is called pre-tribulationalism, more commonly shortened to "pre-trib".

If you hold this position, you believe that the events of *Revelation*, chapters six through nineteen do not concern the church because the church will be gone. The church has been "caught up" to be with Jesus. Although many Christians today are not aware there are other positions than the pre-trib position, this theology was not widely held prior to the twentieth century.

Post-trib

The predominant thinking of the church through most of its history was that the message of *Revelation* was directed at the church, including the church's presence during the Tribulation. This position is known as post-tribulationism, or in shortened form, post-trib. When martyrs and saints are mentioned in the text, this position would contend that the text is talking about Christians. If you hold this position you believe the rapture of the church occurs immediately prior to the second coming of Jesus.

Part of the pre-trib rationale involves the idea that the wrath of God would not be directed against the church. Many who hold a post-trib view would agree with this. But they would point out that part of what is happening during the Tribulation is persecution of the saints by the Anti-Christ. Since the churches to which the original letter was sent were in the midst of tribulation, it would be argued that the purpose of the letter is more consistent with a post-trib theology.

Mid-trib

Although not as popular as either the pre-trib or post-trib positions, some have argued for a mid-tribulation rapture. This theology argues that there is a difference between the first half of the Tribulation and the second half. The second three-and-a-half years are distinguished as the "Great Tribulation" and the "mid-tribber" believes the church will not be subjected to that part of the larger Tribulation.

Interpretive Decisions

When studying *Revelation* there are many moments when you have to make interpretive decisions. The issue of whether the church will go through the Tribulation, or be taken out of the world before it begins, is one of the biggest. I will be coming at the text from a post-trib perspective. I often tell friends that it is the one point in my theology where I hope I'm wrong! At times I will point out how other positions might understand certain parts of the book. Since there are credible options I would encourage all of us to treat these things with a degree of humility.

The Fifth Seal

When he opened the fifth seal, I saw under the altar the souls of those who had been slain, because of the word of God and the testimony they had maintained, (Rev. 6:9).

John watched as Jesus opened the fifth seal. He tells us he saw an altar in Heaven. Specifically, he said he saw what was *under* the altar. In the Old Testament instructions for sacrifice in the Tabernacle, the blood of the sacrificial animal was to be poured out "under the altar." The blood of the sacrificial animal represented the animal's life. In *Leviticus* God told Moses, "The life is in the blood." (Lev. 17:11)

In Heaven, what John sees under the altar are the "souls" of those who have been put to death for their faith in Jesus. These martyrs are those who not only have been "living sacrifices" for Jesus Christ, but they have given their very lives for their faith. They are men and women like Polycarp and Antipas. Symbolically, their lives have been "poured out under the altar" in Heaven.

These martyrs ask a question of Jesus. They want to know how long it will be until God avenges their murders. These men and women are not seeking revenge. They are seeking justice. They ask their question with righteous indignation, knowing that the day is coming when all injustice will be made right.

In response to the question, they are given white robes. They are also told that what they long for is coming. But they are also told that before God executes his final judgment, others will experience martyrdom.

There are two words used to talk about those yet to be killed. One is "fellow servants," which is a translation of the Greek word *doulos*, which Paul used frequently when he referred to himself as a "servant" of Jesus Christ. The other word is "brothers." The Greek word is *adelphos*. Outside of *Revelation*, both of these words are primarily applied to believers. During the Tribulation, it is probably going to cost many Christians their lives to faithfully believe in Christ. The Tribulation period will be much like the time the churches during the first century were experiencing. People will have to confess their allegiance. There will be only two options: Antichrist or Jesus Christ. If you confess Jesus Christ, it will cost you your life.

Cosmic Cataclysm

I watched as he opened the sixth seal. There was a great earthquake. The sun turned black like sackcloth made of goat-hair, the whole moon turned blood-red, and the stars fell to earth as late figs drop from a fig tree when shaken by a strong wind. The sky receded like a scroll, rolling up and every mountain and island was removed from its place, (Rev. 6:12-14).

The opening of the sixth seal unleashes a time of incredible cosmic upheaval. Everything contained in this passage--the earth-quake, the sun being darkened, a blood-red moon, the stars falling from the sky, the sky receding, mountains and islands being removed--all of these events are contained in Old Testament prophecies concerning the coming of the Day of the Lord.

As the first six seals were opened, John received a panoramic view of the Tribulation. It will be a time of conquest. It will be a time of intense warfare. It will be a time of economic collapse accompanied by scarcity. It will be a time when massive numbers of the earth's population perish. It will be a time of martyrdom for the saints. It will be a time of cosmic upheaval, when the earth itself is shaken. Mankind realizes that the end of the world is upon them. With one accord the critical question of the hour is asked, "For the great day of their wrath has come, and who can stand?" (Rev. 6:17) Who can survive the end of the world? That question is anwered in the next chapter.

Chapter Thirteen: *Sealed for Survival*

By the end of the sixth chapter of *Revelation* six of seven seals on the scroll have been opened. The extent of destruction unleashed with the opening of the sixth seal has caused panic on the earth. All the unredeemed hide from God and ask a critical question:

For the great day of their wrath has come, and who can stand? (Rev. 6:17).

The answer to this question is found in the visions contained in chapter seven of *Revelation*. John sees two groups of people who will come through the Tribulation with flying colors. The first is a group of 144,000 people who are "sealed." When you understand the meaning of the seal, and whom these people represent, you will have another piece of the end-times puzzle in place.

The Sealing

Then I saw another angel coming up from the east, having the seal of the living God. He called out in a loud voice ... 'Do not harm the land or the sea or the trees until we put a seal on the foreheads of the servants of our God,' (Rev. 7:1-4).

Chapters six and seven of *Revelation* are rich in Old Testament imagery. Both the four horsemen of chapter six and the four winds of heaven in chapter seven are drawn from a vision Zechariah recorded in the sixth chapter of his prophecy. There we read:

I looked up again, and there before me were four chariots coming out from between two mountains, mountains of bronze! The first chariot had red horses, the second black, the third white, and the fourth dappled--all of them powerful. I asked the angel who was speaking to me, 'What are these, my Lord?' The angel answered me, 'These are the four winds of heaven, going out from standing in the presence of the Lord of the whole world,'" (Zechariah 6:1-5).

An angel tells the prophet that the four horse-drawn chariots are symbolic of the four winds of heaven. The four winds of heaven, which are held back in chapter seven of *Revelation*, could very easily be connected to the four horsemen of chapter six. In both cases judgment is being held back until God removes his restraint.

One characteristic of apocalyptic literature is the way it shifts its symbolism. The same event is not always portrayed in exactly the same way every time. For instance, there are four different visions of Christ in *Revelation*. The vision of Jesus in chapter one, where he appears as the glorified Son of Man is significantly different than the vision of Christ in chapter five, where he is described as a Lamb who comes and takes the scroll from the one seated on the throne. In chapter one we see Christ in glory, with His hair white like wool, his feet glowing like brass, and his eyes burning like fire. In chapter five, he appears as a lamb with seven horns and seven eyes. Both visions are of Christ, but the symbolism has changed.

In the same way the four horsemen potentially can be identified with the four winds, the 144,000 and the Great Multitude of chapter seven could be the same group of people represented by two different symbols. If that is true, then the sealing that takes place in chapter seven actually could precede the events of Chapter six.

The concept of "sealing" first appears in the prophecy of Ezekiel. *Ezekiel* chapters seven and eight contain a report of Israel's idolatry and God's coming judgment because of their idolatry. But, in chapter nine, we are told that something precedes this judgment:

Then the Lord called to the man clothed in linen who had the writing kit at his side and said to him, 'Go throughout the city of Jerusalem and put a mark on the foreheads of those who grieve and lament over all the detestable things that are done in it.'

As I listened he said to the others, 'Follow him through the city and kill, without showing pity or compassion…but do not touch anyone who has the mark,' (Ezek. 9:1-6).

Before God judged the nation of Israel, he "sealed" those who grieved and repented over the sin of Israel. That "seal" provided protection in the midst of the judgment that was coming upon the land. The same image is now shown to John in *Revelation*.

Judgment is coming on the land, but before judgment comes, the seal of the living God is placed on the foreheads of his "servants". Those who are sealed are protected. The answer to the question of chapter 6, "Who can stand?" is that those who have the seal of the living God upon them can, because they will be protected. They are "sealed" for survival.

The Seal

What is this seal? A seal, in the Roman world, was a mark of ownership. When you owned a cow, you put your "seal" on it. As a mark of ownership, a seal declared the fact that you would protect this animal because it belonged to you.

This word "to seal" is used thirty-two times in the New Testament, and twenty-two of those are found here in the *Revelation*. The concept of the seal is another of the major themes of the book. There are two classes of people in the book. There are those who have been sealed by God and bear the mark of the living God. And there are those who bear the mark or the seal of the Beast.

Are these visible or invisible marks? Let's look for a second at the seal of God outside the book of *Revelation*. In Ephesians 1:13 we are told, "When you believed, you were marked in him with a seal, the promised Holy Spirit." Ephesians 4:30 commands, "Do not grieve the Holy Spirit of God, with whom you were sealed for the day of redemption." II Corinthians 1:12-22 tells us, "He anointed us, set his seal of ownership on us, and put his Spirit in our hearts as a deposit guaranteeing what is to come."

Outside of *Revelation*, the believer's seal is the presence of the Holy Spirit in his or her life. Is that visible? We are not like the high priest at the tabernacle who wore a visible plate across his forehead that said, "Holy to the Lord." The "seal" of the living God in *Revelation* seven is symbolic of the presence of the Holy Spirit in a man or woman's life. If I give allegiance to Christ, He seals me. If I give allegiance to the Beast, he marks me. Much of the popular literature on *Revelation* hypothetically proposes that the mark of the Beast will be something like a tattoo or implanted chip. That is certainly possible. But, it is also possible that the "mark of the Beast" is not visible. Believe me, if the bank told me, "We're taking your credit card away, but all you have to do is get a little tattoo on your forehead or chip in your hand," I'd say, "Forget it!" The "mark" could be visible, but it might symbolize the reality in a person's heart that has rejected Christ and chosen to give his or her allegiance to Antichrist. Such a person has already been "sealed" with the mark of the beast, without any outward manifestation whatsoever!

The 144,000

We are told that the people who are sealed consist of "144,000 from all the tribes of Israel." At first glance we would be tempted to take this statement literally. But there are two "Israels" in the Bible. There is national Israel; a geopolitical reality composed of men and women of Jewish descent who live in their ancient homeland. That group is often referred to in the New Testament. If you read *Romans* chapters nine through eleven you will find that Paul makes a definite distinction between the church and national Israel. But, there is another Israel in the Scriptures, and that is spiritual Israel. In *Romans*, the Apostle Paul writes:

A man is not a Jew if he is only one outwardly, nor is circumcision merely outward and physical. No, a man is a Jew if he is one inwardly; and circumcision is circumcision of the heart, by the Spirit, not by the written code, (Romans 2:28-29).

There is an obvious difference between a blood Jew and a spiritual Jew. It is possible to be both, but it is also possible not to be a physical Jew and yet to be a Jew spiritually, because you have been "circumcised" by the Holy Spirit's presence in your life. You then become part of spiritual Israel. In *Galatians*, Paul states, "If you belong to Christ, you are Abraham's seed," (Gal. 3:29). You are a true descendant of Abraham when you come into relationship with Jesus Christ. Paul ends the book of *Galatians* with a very interesting little phrase: "Peace and mercy to all who follow this rule, even the Israel of God," (Gal. 6:16). This is a reference to the church. Those of us who become Abraham's seed, through faith in Jesus Christ, become the true Israel of God. With that piece of data plugged in, lets take another look at the 144,000 of *Revelation* chapter seven.

When you look closely at this list of tribes, you will discover that these are not the original twelve tribes listed in *Genesis*. If you look at chapter forty-nine of *Genesis* you will see that the tribe of Joseph was one of the original twelve tribes of Israel. In Egypt, Joseph had two sons. Their names were Ephraim and Manasseh. Joseph requested that the land that would be given to his descendants be divided between the descendants of his two sons. The two tribes that came from Joseph replaced the tribe of Joseph.

At the time of the conquest of Canaan, there were no longer twelve tribes, but rather thirteen tribes. The tribes listed in *Revelation* are not the tribes of *Genesis,* or of the conquest. In *Ezekiel*, chapter forty-eight, we are given a prophecy of the end times that many would consider a prophecy of the millennial period. The passage tells of the final resettlement of the land of Israel. The list of tribes in *Ezekiel* is not the same list that is found here in *Revelation.*

You will notice that in verse eight, the tribe of Joseph is listed, (Rev. 7:8). If you go back to verse six, you will see the tribe of Manasseh listed. You can read all day long, and you will never find the tribes of Dan or Ephraim listed. We have a peculiarity here! We have an Israel that is not literally Israel!

The order of tribes is also peculiar. This is the only time that the first tribe listed is the tribe of Judah. Judah was the messianic tribe. It was Jesus Christ's own tribe. So, we have an Israel that somehow is not literally Israel; Judah is listed first; and Dan and Ephraim are omitted. We can analyze this information and arrive at two possibilities.

The first possibility is that the 144,000 is not symbolic. It refers to 144,000 Jews. God has kept track of the tribes, and not one Jew from the tribe of Dan or Ephraim has been included. These 144,000, then, are servants of God, but not Christians.

Pre-tribulation interpretations of *Revelation* teach that these are actual Jews who believe in Christ at the beginning of the tribulation period. These Jews become believers and function as God's prophets and evangelists during the tribulation period. In the second half of the chapter, according to this position, the great multitude is said to be the fruit of their ministry.

The second possibility is that the 144,000 is symbolic. This is an Israel that is not a literal Israel; it is a symbolic Israel. This would be the interpretation given to the passage by both post-tribulationists and mid-tribulationists. The 144,000 are symbolic of the church on earth. The church is the true Israel of God. The entire church is sealed by God and protected from his wrath as they go through the tribulation. I believe that both of these views are valid possibilities. Personally, I believe that what we see here is the church on earth, the symbolic Israel, sealed and protected by God, so that they will not suffer the wrath of God during the tribulation period.

The Great Multitude

I looked and there before me was a great multitude that no one could count, from every nation, tribe, people and language, standing before the throne, and in front of the Lamb, (Rev. 7:9).

In chapter six of *Revelation*, when Jesus opened the fifth seal, we saw the martyrs under the altar. When they asked how long until God's righteous judgment was executed on Earth they were told to wait a little longer until the martyrdom of their fellow servants and brothers was completed. Now, in this chapter, we see a great multitude present in heaven and are told that they represent those who have been martyred during the great tribulation, (Rev. 7:14).

Remember, the primary historical message of *Revelation* was one of assurance to Christians suffering persecution at the hands of Caesar. The message that God was communicating to the first century audience was, "You might go through persecution, you might even be martyred, but you will be sealed and protected from my wrath. At the end, when your tribulation is over, you will stand before my throne. You will be mine for all eternity." The message to the first century church was one of assurance and comfort.

The 144,000 and the Great Multitude could be the same group, viewed two different ways. The 144,000 represent the church on earth, sealed by God at the beginning of the tribulation; the Great Multitude represents all believers, standing before the throne of God at the end of the age. This vision flashes from the beginning of the Tribulation all the way to the end in one chapter. The 144,000 represent the church militant; sealed and protected from God's wrath. The great multitude represents the church triumphant: victorious over Antichrist's persecution. The message of *Revelation* is that if we do suffer martyrdom, we will be victors, because of the Lamb. We will ultimately stand before Him, clothed in white, welcomed in His presence. In the end of the beginning, all will be well.

When he opened the seventh seal, there was silence in Heaven for about half an hour. And I saw the seven angels who stand before God, and to them were given seven trumpets, (Rev. 8:1-2).

Chapter eight of *Revelation* begins with Jesus opening the seventh and final seal on the scroll. As the scroll is opened the focus shifts back to the throne of God in Heaven. John saw seven angels who were given seven trumpets. The sounding of these trumpets will produce an intensification of God's purifying and redemptive judgment. Before these trumpets were sounded, however, John was given another vision that helps us understand the seven trumpet judgments.

John saw the true Tabernacle in Heaven. There in the Tabernacle, he saw an altar. In the Tabernacle on earth, the altar of incense stood before the curtain that separated the Holy Place from the Holy of Holies. In the earthly Tabernacle, the altar of incense symbolized that prayer was the means of access into the Holy of Holies; where God manifested his presence.

The same is true in Heaven. John wrote, "The smoke of the incense, along with the prayers of the saints, went up before God from the angel's hands," (Rev. 8:4). It was the specific content of these prayers that produced the events of the trumpet judgments.

Throughout the centuries Christians have prayed the Lord's Prayer. Jesus taught us to pray that his kingdom would come, and that His will would be done on earth as it is in Heaven. Throughout the centuries those prayers for the coming of God's kingdom have ascended before God's throne. The answer to those prayers involves seven angels with seven trumpets. When the seventh angel sounds his trumpet, loud voices in heaven will proclaim, "The kingdom of the world has become the kingdom of our Lord and of his Christ," (Rev. 11:15).

Picture what this message meant to a Christian going through persecution at the time John was writing this letter. Believers were being put to death for their faith in Jesus; they saw unrighteousness triumphing in incredible ways as a satanic emperor sat on the throne in Rome. The power of Rome seemed unbreakable. The saints were crushed, persecuted, and martyred for their faith. They were probably crying out to God, "God, don't you hear our prayers? Vindicate your righteousness. Judge the wicked; save your people." The book of *Revelation* affirms that those prayers will be answered!

Seven Trumpets

The trumpet is a vivid symbol throughout the Bible. Since the time the trumpet sounded to announce the presence of God at Sinai (Ex. 19), the sounding of the trumpet has been a biblical symbol of divine intervention in human history.

There are many different philosophies in the world today. The materialist says there is no God; we live in a mechanistic universe. Therefore, everything that happens in the universe is a process of cause and effect within a closed system. Everything can be explained by natural causes.

The deist believes in a Supreme Being who set the whole system into motion, and then stepped aside. Everything again operates on the principle of cause and effect in a closed system; therefore, everything can still be explained in terms of natural law and order.

The biblical theist believes there is a Creator who did set the universe in motion. He affirms that God does use natural laws and natural order and that there is a system of cause and effect. But, he also knows that God is not limited by a closed system. The system is open. At any time, the God who created the universe, set it into motion, and actually created the laws of natural order, can intervene in the system. The trumpet is the symbol of such divine intervention.

Each of the trumpet judgments introduces us to a source of destruction, the object of destruction, and the extent of destruction. Each trumpet requires an interpretive decision regarding how you are going to understand the judgment. For instance, when the first angel sounds his trumpet judgment is unleashed upon the earth. The source of destruction is hail and fire, mixed with blood. The objects of destruction are the earth, the trees, and the green grass. The extent of destruction is one-third of all these resources. The decision that has to be made is whether this is a literal destruction of one third of the earth, or whether it is symbolic of something else.

When the second angel sounds his trumpet judgment us unleashed on the sea. The source of destruction is a mountain that is cast into the sea. One-third of the sea turns into blood, one-third of the creatures in the sea die, and one-third of the ships of the sea are destroyed. We have to ask ourselves the question: "Is this the literal destruction of one-third of the sea, or is it symbolic?"

When the third trumpet sounds, a great falling star, named Wormwood, turns one-third of the rivers and one-third of the springs of water "bitter." To be "bitter" means the water becomes poisonous. People die from the bitter waters. A decision has to be made. Is this a literal destruction of one third of the rivers and waters, or is it symbolic?

When the fourth angel sounds his trumpet, one-third of the light of the sun, moon, and stars is turned dark. One-third of the day is without light, and one-third of the night is without light. Again, we have to make a decision. Is this a literal destruction of one-third of the heavenly bodies, or is this symbolic?

The fifth trumpet is called the first "Woe." The exclamation "Woe!" was a common part of the Old Testament prophet's vocabulary. When the prophet spoke of judgment coming upon the land, he would preface his remarks with the phrase, "Woe to you!"

When the fifth and sixth angels blow their trumpets there is an intensification of judgment. When the fifth trumpet sounds, a fallen star is given a key, an abyss is opened and locusts with the sting of scorpions come out of the abyss. Men without God's seal are tortured for five months. We have a decision to make. Are these literal creatures, or are they symbolic?

The sixth trumpet sounding ushers in the second "Woe". Four angels who are bound at the Euphrates River are released. These angels restrain two hundred million mounted troops! When these troops are released one-third of earth's population is killed. We have a decision to make; is this literally two hundred million soldiers that kill one third of mankind, or is it symbolic?

The seals, the trumpets, and the bowls are probably the most difficult part of *Revelation* to understand. We know that John is supposed to be writing in symbolic language, but sometimes he seems to be speaking literally. It is very difficult to determine exactly when he is speaking literally and when he is speaking symbolically. Let's see what this passage might teach if it is first taken very "literally," and then interpreted symbolically.

"Literal" Interpretation
There are some who would interpret these things "literally."

I have talked to pastors who are absolutely convinced that the first five trumpets portray events that would happen in a nuclear holocaust. According to this interpretive scheme, the first trumpet represents the first blast of a nuclear explosion. In that blast, one third of the earth is destroyed. The potential now exists for one third of the earth's surface to be easily destroyed by the initial exchange in a nuclear war.

The second and third trumpets are the results of radiation fall-out. Through radiation poisoning, the oceans and all the fresh water supplies are severely damaged.

The fourth trumpet, which darkens a third of the sun, the moon, and the stars, would be caused by the debris from the explosions entering the atmosphere. The debris would cut the amount of light that comes from these heavenly bodies by a third.

The fifth trumpet, the locusts of the pit, would represent the effects of radiation poisoning. The same two statements that are made here in the book of *Revelation* are the two statements that people made about the effects of radiation poisoning at Hiroshima and Nagasaki. It was said that the pain of radiation poisoning was like the sting of a scorpion, and that people actually sought to die because the pain was so intense.

In the literal scheme, the sixth trumpet would represent the beginning of Armageddon. The angels remove their restraint and the two-hundred million man army of the Kings of the East moves into the Middle East.

This kind of a "literal" view could all be fulfilled in our day through a nuclear war. But even in this approach much of the interpretation is based on symbolism.

A Symbolic Interpretation

The first trumpet judgment leads to the destruction of one-third of the earth. In a symbolic interpretation, the "one-third" figure would represent that the destruction is not total. When we get to the bowl judgments, we're going to see that many of the judgments of the trumpets are repeated, but with a totally destructive intensity. Since the earth is the means of production in John's day, in the same way the Nile was the means of production at the time of the Exodus, those holding a more symbolic view see the destruction of one-third of the earth as partial destruction of the means of production. If this is true, we have a correlation with the economic collapse that took place when the third seal was opened.

The second trumpet, the mountain falling into the sea, contains an allusion to *Jeremiah* 51:24-25. There, Babylon is viewed as a "mountain" that destroys the whole earth. The Jeremiah passage talks about how God is going to destroy Babylon. In the book of *Revelation*, "Babylon" is consistently a symbol of a godless world system. The sea symbolizes the Gentile nations. The second trumpet might symbolize the destructive influence of the world system in the last days.

The third trumpet, the star called Wormwood, fits well within this scheme. Consistently, we have seen that stars symbolize angels. A great fallen star can be symbolic of a powerful fallen demonic spirit. Wormwood means "bitterness." In the Old Testament, the poisonous nature of false religion and idolatry was called "wormwood" or "bitterness." Waters are symbolic of spiritual systems.

In *John* chapter four, Jesus spoke of himself as living water. In *John* chapter seven, Jesus said, "If any one is thirsty, let him come to me, and drink." The waters of *Revelation* eight might be symbolic of spiritual systems and philosophies.

Symbolically, this trumpet would represent the poisonous influence that penetrates the godless philosophies of men, and the idolatrous and false religious systems that destroy mankind. Darkness and light are consistent biblical images of truth and error. The darkness of the fourth trumpet would then symbolize the spiritual confusion produced in the minds of men through the influence of such faulty teaching, philosophies, and spiritual deception.

The fifth trumpet produces an all-out release of demonic activity. The abyss that is referred to here was the prison abode of fallen angels. The fifth trumpet potentially represents the release of vast waves of demonic activity.

A real locust lives on green plants. These locusts are told not to eat any green things. Instead, they live by tormenting people. In the same way that a locust feeds upon the green things of the earth and can only survive by devouring them, these demonic personalities live by tormenting people's lives. They thrive upon destruction. Believers are sealed against this trumpet. Only unbelievers are affected by this unleashing of the forces of hell. Very appropriately, the one having authority over these forces is named Abaddon or Apollyon, meaning "Destroyer" or

"Destruction." The destruction of people's lives is the product of a fallen world system.

Continual tribulation

As you study *Revelation* you must remember that there is a sense in which the Tribulation is simply the logical outcome of the tribulation that God's people have faced throughout human history. Tribulation has been part of church history from the ascension of Jesus Christ to the present times. In *Revelation*, tribulation intensifies and reaches its climax in the end times. The seal judgments possibly represent the natural course of the present age reaching its logical conclusion. With the trumpets, God intervenes and removes His restraining power. This allows the demonic world system to reach its logical outcome. Then in the bowl judgments God pours out the full fury of His wrath on that system. Either way you interpret this passage, whether as the literal destruction of the earth, or as the unleashing of spiritual forces of destruction, the passage paints a terrifying picture of life on earth during this period of time called the Tribulation. We may never exactly understand these events until they happen. But there are two definite lessons we can learn from this passage.

The first lesson is that judgment comes in response to the prayers of the saints. Our prayers are effectual in producing God's righteous purposes. The second lesson we learn is the response of people living on the earth who do not know Christ during this period of time:

The rest of mankind that were not killed by these plagues still did not repent of the work of their hands; they did not stop worshipping demons and idols of gold, silver, bronze, stone and wood...Nor did they repent of their murders, their sorceries, their sexual immorality or their thefts. (Rev. 9:20-21)

Even in the midst of what must surely be recognized as divine judgment, unredeemed humanity does not repent. God executes judgment to bring people to repentance; but there is none. God is righteous when He judges, and judge He will!

CHAPTER FIFTEEN: *Scrolls and Witnesses*

Then I saw another mighty angel coming down from Heaven. He was robed in a cloud, with a rainbow above his head; his face was like the sun, and his legs were like fiery pillars, (Rev. 10:1).

The message of the angel

When the next chapter of *Revelation* opens, six of the seven trumpets have sounded. In the same way that there was an interlude between the opening of the sixth and seventh seals, chapter ten of *Revelation* contains a break between the sixth and seventh trumpets.

The chapter begins with John having a vision of what he called "a mighty angel". The description of this angel is very similar to the description of an angel Daniel saw Babylon:

On the 24th day of the first month, as I was standing on the bank of the great river, the Tigris, I looked up and there before me was a man dressed in linen, with a belt of the finest gold around his waist. His body was like chrysolite, his face like lightning, his eyes like flaming torches, his arms and legs like the gleam of burnished bronze, and his voice like the sound of a multitude, (Dan. 10:4-6).

This angel was sent to Daniel with a message. He told Daniel:

At that time Michael, the great prince who protects your people, will arise. There will be a time of distress such as has not happened from the beginning of nations until then, (Daniel 12:1).

The angel's message concerned the coming of the Great Tribulation. In much the same way, the angel in *Revelation* revealed to John a similar message. John said this angel was standing with one foot on the land and one foot on the sea. The angel proclaimed a simple, yet profound message: "There will be no more delay!" (Rev. 10:6).

There has been a divine delay in the second coming of Jesus Christ. Some thirty years prior to the time *Revelation* was written, the Apostle Peter wrote a letter contained in our New Testament under the title *II Peter.* In Peter's day, Christians were being mocked because of their belief in the second coming of Christ. Peter wrote:

The Lord is not slow in keeping his promise, as some understand slowness. He is patient with you, not wanting anyone to perish, but everyone to come to repentance, (II Peter 2:8).

There is a divine delay. Peter went on to write:

But the day of the Lord will come like a thief. The heavens will disappear with a roar; the elements will be destroyed by fire, and the earth and everything in it will be laid bare, (II Peter 2:10).

The message of this angel was that the delay is over. When the seventh trumpet sounds, God's ultimate purposes will be accomplished.

The Seven Thunders Speak

In the midst of this vision, John says that this angel gave a loud shout that was like the roar of a lion. Then he tells us that when the angel shouted "the voices of the seven thunders spoke." When John started to write down what the "thunders" said, he was told by a voice from heaven not to write what he heard.

This little piece of information is baffling. First, we are not given any kind of hint of what the "seven thunders" are. Then we are left wondering what they said. Like Daniel at the time of his vision, John is told to "seal up" what was said. I find it refreshing that there are some things we are just not meant to know until the time is right.

The Little Scroll

Go take the scroll that lies open in the hand of the angel who is standing on the sea and on the land, (Rev. 10:8).

John said that the voice from Heaven then instructed him to take the scroll from the hand of this angel and eat it. This scroll contains the events that will occur when the seventh angel sounds the seventh trumpet. It is the message of the final judgment of God upon the unbelieving world.

The prophet Ezekiel received a similar message. In *Ezekiel,* the prophecy of the judgment coming upon the nation of Israel was contained in a scroll. The prophet was instructed to eat the scroll and then to speak to the house of Israel, (Ez. 3:1). To "eat a scroll" involved receiving a message from God that in turn was proclaimed. John ate the scroll. After eating the scroll, he was told, "You must prophesy again about many peoples, nations, languages, and kings," (Rev. 10:11).

When John ate the scroll it was sweet to the taste. But after he had eaten the scroll it turned sour in his stomach. The primary message of the scroll is that Jesus Christ is coming again. That is sweet to the taste. But, the message is also sour to the stomach because of what the second coming of Christ involves. It involves a time of intense judgment upon the world. What at first might seem "sweet" is also "sour". The Tribulation is going to be a terrifying experience for those who do not know Jesus Christ.

The prophet Zephaniah expressed the same truth:

The great day of the Lord is near--near and coming quickly. Listen! The cry on the day of the Lord will be bitter, the shouting of the warrior there. That day will be a day of wrath, a day of distress and anguish, a day of trouble and ruin, a day of darkness and gloom, a day of clouds and blackness, a day of trumpet and battle cry against the fortified, cities and against the corner towers. I will bring distress on the people and they will walk like blind men, because they have sinned against the Lord. Their blood will be poured out like dust and their entrails like filth. Neither their silver nor their gold will be able to save them on the day of the Lord's wrath. In the fire of his jealousy the whole world will be consumed, for he will make a sudden end of all who live in the earth," (Zeph.1:14-18).

The message is sweet to the taste, but it is bitter to the stomach!

Two Witnesses

After eating the scroll, John was given a measuring device and told to measure the Temple, (Rev. 11:1). He was also told about two witnesses that would prophesy and then be martyred in the streets of Jerusalem. This is another point where an interpretive decision needs to be made. Are these things literal...or symbolic.

If literal, then the passage refers to two literal people and a literal temple. When John received this vision the Temple in Jerusalem was gone. In 70 A.D., after a three-year siege, the Roman general Titus breached the walls of Jerusalem and destroyed the Temple.

If John is told to go and measure the temple, and the passage is literal, then the Temple will need to be rebuilt in the last days. There is a great deal of disagreement about whether it is necessary for the Temple to be rebuilt before Jesus comes again. Even the Jewish people are in disagreement about the importance of building a third Temple. The majority of Jews in Israel today are secular. They view the destiny of the restored nation as a matter of military superiority. As hostile Arab nations surround them, they live in a perpetual state of armed readiness.

Those who are conservative, and religious, believe the hope of Israel is the coming of the Messiah. They don't believe Jesus was the Messiah. They believe that before Messiah comes, the Temple must be rebuilt. In order for that to happen, the Muslim Dome of the Rock, the second holiest spot in Islam, must be removed.

For John to measure a literal temple, either that Dome must be destroyed, or archeologists must find that the original Temple was built at a location that allows a new Temple to be rebuilt without the Dome being destroyed. Keep your eyes on the Temple Mount in the days to come!

There have been many theories concerning the two witnesses. If they are two actual people, some speculate they are Elijah and Enoch. In the Old Testament, both Enoch and Elijah were caught up to heaven without experiencing physical death.

Enoch is a mysterious character. He is mentioned briefly in *Genesis*, (Genesis 5:24). In the New Testament book of *Jude*, we are told that Enoch was a prophet:

Enoch, the seventh from Adam, prophesied about these men: See, the Lord is coming with thousands upon thousands of his holy ones to judge everyone, and to convict all of them of all the ungodly acts they have committed in their ungodliness, and of all the defiant words ungodly sinners have spoken against him., (Jude 14).

Elijah is a good candidate, not only because he was taken to Heaven without dying, but also because of what we are told about him in the Old Testament. The next to the last verse of the Old Testament says, "See, I will send you the prophet Elijah before the great and dreadful day of the Lord comes," (Malachi 4:5).

Others who believe the witnesses are two literal people propose they are Elijah and Moses. It was Elijah and Moses that appeared to Jesus on the Mount of Transfiguration and spoke with Him about the things that were to come, (Luke 9:30-31).

The miraculous powers attributed to the two witnesses are very similar to those exhibited during the ministries of Elijah and Moses. We are told the these men will have power to shut up the sky so that it will not rain during the time they are prophesying. Elijah had this same ability during the reign of King Ahab (See Kings chapter 17). They also have the power to turn water into blood and to strike the earth with plagues. This parallels the events of the ministry of Moses at the time of the Exodus.

What is the function of these two witnesses? We are told they will minister as prophets for three-and-a-half years with great power. After this period of ministry they will be killed by Antichrist in Jerusalem. The entire world will celebrate their deaths:

For 3 1/2 days men from every people, tribe, language and nation will gaze on their bodies and refuse them burial. The inhabitants of the earth will gloat over them and will celebrate by sending each other gifts, because these two prophets had tormented those who live on the earth, (Rev. 11:9-10).

At the end of three-and-a-half days the two are going to be resurrected and then caught up to Heaven. Then a severe earthquake will strike Jerusalem and seven thousand people are going to die, (Rev. 11:9-13).

If you take a non-symbolic approach to the passage it looks like this: There will be two men whom God will raise up in the end times to be prophets to an unrighteous world; they will prophesy for three-and-a-half years with the power of Moses and Elijah (or perhaps they will be Moses and Elijah); and at the end of those three-and-a-half years, Antichrist will murder them. They will lie dead for three-and-a-half days before the watching world. God will raise them from the dead and snatch them up into heaven. That is one way this passage can be interpreted.

But what if this vision is symbolic? The passage begins with the measuring of a temple. The Bible says the you and I are now the temple of God, (I Cor. 3:6-7). The church is now the temple of God. The temple in this vision might be the church portrayed symbolically.

There are two different Greek words translated "temple." There is a word that speaks of the entire temple complex, including the court of Gentiles, the court of the women, and the outer court. But there is also a word, which speaks specifically of the sanctuary

- the Holy Place and the Holy of Holies. That is the Greek word *naos,* which is used here. This word refers to that part of the temple where the presence of God was manifested. When the Holy Spirit comes to indwell a man or woman they become the temple of God. If this passage is symbolic, the temple represents the church.

Throughout the Bible, when a prophet was told to measure something, it was measured either as a symbol of destruction or as a symbol of preservation. The measuring of the temple here very possibly is referring to the protective "sealing" of the church. While the temple is measured, the outer court is not measured. The outer court was the area Gentiles were allowed to enter. The church is sealed, but the rest of the world is trampled under, i.e. is judged during the Tribulation.

There are a variety of options concerning the symbolism of the two witnesses. Some scholars believe they represent the law and the prophets. Others believe they symbolize the Old Testament and the New Testament. Still others believe they are symbolic of the people of God, Old Testament and New Testament. The significance of "two witnesses" is taken from the Old Testament law in *Deuteronomy.* There we read that a true and valid testimony required two reliable witnesses, (Dt. 1:15). The two witnesses would symbolize the faithful witness by God's people in the last days.

These witnesses are called "the two olive trees and the two lampstands that stand before the Lord of the earth," (Rev. 11:4). This is a direct quote from the book of *Zechariah.* Zechariah was given a vision concerning the rebuilding of the temple at the time of the return from captivity. The prophet was instructed to tell Zerubbabel, the man in charge of the construction, that God's way of the rebuilding the Temple would be, "Not by might, nor by power, but by my Spirit," (Zechariah 4: 6).

Zechariah had a vision of a lampstand and two olive trees. The oil from the olive trees was flowing into the candlesticks to fuel them. What do lampstands represent in the book of *Revelation?* The church. What does oil represent in the New Testament? The Holy Spirit. Symbolically, the two witnesses represent the church witnessing in the power of the Holy Spirit in the last days.

The temple and the two witnesses are symbols of the church. The temple symbolizes the church in worship, sealed and protected. The two witnesses symbolize the church in ministry.

These are the two primary functions of the church in every age: worship and witness. Worship alone is inadequate; witness alone is inadequate.

This vision is symbolic of the church's worldwide ministry during the Tribulation. Believers will witness in the power of Elijah and Moses. The time of the greatest spiritual effectiveness in church history will come in the time of the greatest persecution the church has ever known. Historically, this has always been the case. Under pressure, the church flourishes.

We are told that no one can harm these two during this time. "If anyone tries to harm them, fire comes from their mouths and devours their enemies," (Rev. 11:5). This promise is similar to what God said to Jeremiah, "I will make my words in your mouth a fire and these people the wood it consumes," (Jer. 5:14). The fire in their mouth that devours their enemies is simply the message of God's coming judgment.

There is a direct parallel here with what we saw earlier in the book. The temple sealed and protected here parallels the 144,000 who were sealed and protected in chapter seven. The two witnesses martyred here parallel the multitude who have "come out of the Great Tribulation, and have washed their robes in the blood of the Lamb."

When the two witnesses are resurrected, intense judgment is about to fall on the world. The seventh angel sounds his trumpet, and loud voices in heaven proclaim. "The kingdom of the world has become the kingdom of our Lord and of his Christ," (Rev. 11:15).

This entire chapter can be viewed in one of two ways. On the one hand, there might be two men whom God raises up during the Tribulation to have this unique ministry. On the other, this is probably a message to the church.

In chapter six of Revelation, six seals were opened and the question was asked, "Who can stand? Who can survive the end of the world?" The answer was given in Revelation chapter 7--"Those who are sealed for survival." In chapters 8 and 9, six trumpets blow again; there is incredible tribulation. The question could again be asked, "Who can survive? How can we survive?" The answer is given in chapter 11. There is a "temple" which God will have "measured." He will seal it and protect it. There are "two witnesses" who have a ministry. They will prophesy in the power of Elijah and Moses. No one can harm them until their ministry is finished. In the end, they will be martyred, but they will be raised. Ultimately, they will be victorious. So will the church!

CHAPTER SIXTEEN: *From Here to Eternity*

A great sign appeared in heaven: a woman clothed with the sun, with the moon under her feet and a crown of twelve stars on her head. She was pregnant and cried out in pain as she was about to give birth, (Rev. 12:1-2).

Throughout John's vision on the island of Patmos, a consistent pattern emerged regarding the events of the last days. John was shown that two parallel threads would run throughout this period of history. The last days would be characterized by the judgment of God being executed upon an unbelieving world. The Kingdom of God will crush the City of Man. In the midst of God's judgment one group of men and women will be protected. God will "seal" His people.

The other theme that can be traced throughout the book is the persecution that God's people will experience in the last days. In chapter twelve of *Revelation* Jesus showed John why this pattern exists. It is a vision that interprets human history from a spiritual perspective.

The Woman and the Dragon

John wrote that he saw "a great and wondrous sign" appear in Heaven. The word that is translated "wondrous sign" takes us back to the first chapter of *Revelation.* In the Greek, the word that is used here is *semeion,* which has the same root as the word translated "signify" in chapter 1. To "signify" means to communicate a truth in symbols or signs. The word used here speaks of the symbol or sign itself. When John tells us that "a great and wondrous sign appeared", we ought to immediately be on the alert, realizing that these things are highly symbolic.

John saw a woman. She was clothed with the sun, the moon is under her feet, and a crown of twelve stars is on her head. This symbol is taken directly from a dream that the young Joseph had in the book of *Genesis.* In *Genesis* we read:

Then he had another dream and he told it to his brothers. 'Listen,' he said, 'I had another dream, and this time the sun, and moon and eleven stars were bowing down to me," (Genesis 37:9).

When he told his father and brothers about the dream Jacob

rebuked him, and said:

'What is this dream you had? Will your mother and I and your brothers actually come and bow down to the ground before you?' (Gen. 37:10).

The sun, the moon, and the stars symbolized Joseph's mother, father, and brothers. From these twelve brothers came the twelve tribes of the nation of Israel. When we see a woman clothed with the sun, with the moon under her feet, and a crown of twelve stars on her head, we can safely say that symbolically she represents Israel. The problem is, does the symbol represent national Israel or spiritual Israel?

In *Romans*, the Apostle Paul addressed the interrelationship of Israel and the church. Paul raised some critical questions concerning the fate of the nation of Israel. He asked whether they had failed so badly that God had written them off? In that case all the promises made to Israel would now be fulfilled in the church. Paul wrote:

After all, if your were cut out of an olive tree that is wild by nature, and contrary to nature were grafted into a cultivated olive tree, how much more readily will these,   the natural branches, be grafted into their own olive tree?" (Rom. 11:24).

This statement would indicate that God is not finished with national Israel. Picture the whole tree as the people of God. National Israel composed the branches of that tree in the Old Testament. Through their rejection of Jesus, they were broken off. They no longer held the place of being uniquely the people of God. The gentile church was grafted in. The door to becoming the people of God was thrown wide open, and God said, "Whosoever will may come." Believing gentiles became part of the people of God.

Remember that the church was primarily Jewish until the tenth chapter of the book of *Acts*. Then the message began to spread to the non-Jewish world. The New Testament teaches that the wall that divided Jew and Gentile has been broken down so that now we are one new man; we are one people of God, Jew and Gentile, when we come to faith in Christ.

Several passages in the Bible teach that in the end times there will be a spiritual revival among people who belong to national Israel. Many Jewish men and women will come to believe in Jesus as Messiah. These Jews will be "grafted" back into the "tree". When this happens, the people of God will be composed of both the church and believing, national Israel. In *Revelation*, there is no distinction being made between national, believing Israel and the church. The message of *Revelation* is addressed to the people of God as a whole.

But notice that there is a small difference between the image in *Revelation* and the image in Joseph's dream. In *Genesis*, Joseph sees eleven stars bowing down to him. In *Revelation*, the woman's crown has twelve stars. These small changes often have large significance.

As was the case with the 144,000, we have an "Israel" that is not quite "Israel". Here, the woman is not just symbolic of national Israel, but of the people of God throughout the ages; national Israel in the Old Testament; spiritual Israel in the New Testament.

John goes on to say that he saw another "sign". It was an enormous dragon:

Then another sign appeared in heaven: an enormous red dragon with seven heads and ten horns and seven crowns on his heads," (Rev. 12:3).

The dragon is one of the symbols in *Revelation* that the book itself identifies. In verse nine of this chapter we are told the dragon is Satan. The significance of the dragon's horns and crowns will be explored in the next chapter when we will look at the vehicle through which Satan will work in the end times.

Verse four tells us that the dragon's tail swept a third of the stars out of the sky and flung them to the earth. We already know that stars symbolize angels in *Revelation*. A third of the angels of heaven were "flung to the earth." The Bible is not totally explicit about Satan's origins, but there are several passages that give us some "behind the scenes" hints.

In the book of *Isaiah* a prophecy was being directed against Babylon. The immediate message concerned the King of Babylon at the time. But in the middle of the passage something changes. Suddenly Isaiah begins to talk about a person that supersedes the actual King:

How you have fallen from heaven, O morning star, son of the dawn! You have been cast down to the earth, you who once laid low the nations! You said in your heart, 'I will ascend to heaven; I will raise my throne above the stars of God; I will sit enthroned on the mount of assembly, on the utmost heights of the sacred mountain. I will ascend above the tops of the clouds; I will make myself like the Most High.' But you are brought down to the grave, to the depths of the pit," (Isaiah 14:12-15).

Some scholars believe this is a reference to the fall of Lucifer, the angel we call Satan or the Devil, and the origins of evil. In *Ezekiel* chapter twenty-eight we encounter a similar type of situation where a prophecy was directed against the ruler of Tyre. Again, a shift takes place:

You were the model of perfection, full of wisdom and perfect in beauty. You were in Eden, the garden of God; every precious stone adorned you: ruby, topaz and emerald, crysolite, onyx and jasper, sapphire, turquoise and beryl. Your settings and mountings were made of gold; on the day you were created they were prepared. You were anointed as a guardian cherub, for so I ordained you. You were on the holy mount of God; you walked among the fiery stones. You were blameless in your ways from the day you were created until wickedness was found in you,'" (Ezekiel 28:12-15).

This passage is obviously not talking about a human ruler. If it refers to Satan then we learn he was an extremely powerful, intelligent, beautiful angel: the highest of the created order of God's angels. In the same way that man has freedom of will, the angelic beings were given freedom. Lucifer (Satan's proper name) used his freedom to decide to rebel against God. Not content to serve God, Lucifer wanted to be God.

Five times in the *Isaiah* passage Lucifer said, "I will." The essence of sin is the exaltation of self to the position that only God has the right to hold. This passage in *Revelation* suggests that when Lucifer fell, one-third of the angelic host chose to rebel with him. They became fallen angels: the satanic and demonic forces in the world today. These are the principalities and powers, the spiritual forces of wickedness in the heavenly realms, of which Paul speaks in *Ephesians* chapter six.

In John's vision, Satan stood in front of the woman who was

about to give birth so that he could destroy her child the moment it was born, (Rev. 12:4). The dragon pursued the woman and tried to destroy her. Satan's primary activity in the world today is his attempt to destroy the people of God.

In John's day, the people of God were confronted by a world power that was seeking to destroy them. It was the Roman Empire. In *Revelation* God gave them a look behind the scenes at the real source of that persecution. They were the woman. They were the people of God in their generation. The Roman Empire was trying to destroy them. But behind the Roman Empire was the dragon.

The male child

She gave birth to a son, a male child, who "will rule all the nations with an iron scepter." And her child was snatched up to God and to his throne, (Rev. 12:5).

Much of the Old Testament can be understood in light of the fact that the dragon seeks to destroy this male child. The child is Jesus Christ. Throughout ancient history, Satan tried to destroy the coming Messiah. In *Genesis*, after the serpent deceived Adam and Eve, God spoke to the serpent and cursed him:

I will put enmity between you and the woman, and between your seed and hers; he will crush your head, and you will strike his heel, (Gen. 3:15).

Long before Jesus came, the Jewish rabbis recognized this as the first promise of a Messiah. God would send a male child that would crush the serpent. The serpent would strike the male child's heel, but the male child would eventually crush the serpent's head, dealing him a fatal blow.

The Old Testament is filled with examples of Satan trying to destroy the one who would ultimately destroy him. Why did Cain kill Abel? Abel was the righteous seed. The people of God, and eventually Messiah, were to come through the line of Abel. Cain murdered him. In John's gospel, Jesus said that the Devil was a liar and a murderer from the beginning, (John 8:44). Satan motivated Cain to kill Abel. The dragon was seeking to devour the male child.

Who was the power behind Pharaoh in Egypt? The Jews were

becoming too numerous. Pharaoh decided to kill every male child that was born. The dragon was seeking to devour the male child.

Who was the power behind Haman, in Persia? Haman manipulated King Xerxes to issue a decree to have all the Jews in all the provinces where Xerxes reigned murdered. The dragon was seeking to devour the male child. Who was the power behind Herod when he decided to kill all the male babies two years and under in Bethlehem? How can you explain three million Christians being martyred in the first three centuries of church history? How can you explain six million Jews murdered by Hitler? How do you explain the persecution against Christians and Jews around the world today? Behind the scenes, the dragon pursues the woman and her child. Satan seeks to destroy the people of God.

War in Heaven

Then war broke out in heaven. Michael and his angels fought against the dragon, and the dragon and his angels fought back. But he was not strong enough, and they lost their place in heaven. The great dragon was hurled down—that ancient serpent called the devil, or Satan, who leads the whole world astray. He was hurled to the earth, and his angels with him, (Rev. 12:7-9).

The fatal blow to Satan, first prophesied in *Genesis*, was delivered by Jesus at the cross of Calvary. We are still engaged in spiritual warfare, and Satan is our enemy, but we are fighting a defeated foe. Paul wrote:

And having disarmed the power and authorities, he made a public spectacle of them, triumphing over them by the cross, (Colossians 2:15).

John wrote:

The reason the Son of God appeared was to destroy the devil's work, (I John 3:8).

The author of Hebrews wrote:

Since the children have flesh and blood, he too shared in their humanity so that by his death he might destroy him who holds the power of death, that is, the devil, (Heb. 2:14).

Jesus Christ defeated Satan at the cross. For over 2,000 years, for reasons we cannot completely understand, Satan has been given freedom to "ply his trade." God has allowed it. But at the end of time, what has already been accomplished at the cross will be consummated!

Revelation portrays the progressive downfall of Satan. He began as one of the highest of the archangels. His dwelling place was in that realm of the heavenlies called the third heaven. After he sinned, he was cast out of the presence of God and limited to the heavenly realms; what is sometimes called the second heavens. At this point in *Revelation*, we see Satan cast out of the heavenly realms and limited to Earth. Here, for a short season, he will wreak havoc.

Later In *Revelation* Satan is bound for a thousand years in the abyss. Finally, he is cast into the Lake of Fire where he experiences eternal punishment and torment. The message of *Revelation* is that in spite of the way things might look, evil will be overcome in the end! Satan will ultimately be defeated and destroyed!

Here in *Revelation*, when Satan's activities are limited, all of his vengeance is channeled into the single task of trying to annihilate the people of God. As well as revealing to us the role Satan has played throughout history, this chapter also tells us of Satan's most effective tactics:

Now have come the salvation and the power and the kingdom of our God, and the authority of his Messiah. For the accuser of our brothers and sisters, who accuses them before our God day and night, has been hurled down, (Rev. 12:10).

Satan is called "the accuser of our brothers and sisters." You can call Satan the accuser of the brothers and sisters, and Jesus Christ their advocate. Satan constantly accuses us; Jesus Christ constantly stands in our behalf and defends us. One of Satan's most effective schemes is the production of guilt and condemnation through accusation.

Many Christians suffer from guilt and condemnation. Yet, the Bible says, "There is therefore no condemnation for those who are in Christ Jesus," (Romans 8:1). If I sin, God convicts me. The job of the Holy Spirit is conviction, not condemnation. When I confess my sin, the Bible says that God forgives me and cleanses me of all unrighteousness, (I John 1:9). If I go back to God with the same sin again He says, "What are you talking about; I don't even remember that. I have removed your sin as far as the east is from the west," (See Ps. 103). Who then keeps reminding us of the sins which God has already forgiven and forgotten? Satan. He is the accuser of the brethren (both brothers and sisters).

Revelation gives us three clear principles of how we can overcome Satan's schemes. We are told in this chapter that the brothers overcame him: 1) by the blood of the Lamb, 2) by the word of their testimony, and 3) because they did not love their lives so much that they would not even shrink from death, (Rev. 12:11).

The blood of the Lamb speaks of absolute dependence on the life of Christ. His blood represents His life. If we are ever going to be effective in the Christian life, it will be when we realize that we can never live the Christian life with our own limited resources. We must depend upon the power and the resources of the indwelling Christ.

They also overcame him by the word of their testimony. The verbal witness of believers defeats Satan. Finally, they overcame by having a totally abandoned life. If my life is totally abandoned to Jesus Christ, I do not have to worry about Satan's attacks. We are most vulnerable to demonic schemes when we step out of fellowship with Christ. We are also vulnerable in those areas that we are unwilling to relinquish to the lordship of Christ. An abandoned life overcomes Satan.

Divine Protection

When the dragon saw that he had been hurled to the earth, he pursued the woman who had given birth to the male child, (Rev. 12:13).

An intense period of persecution follows Satan being hurled to earth. We are told that he will pursue the woman that gave birth to the child. In the Greek, the word *dioko* means both to pursue and to persecute. Persecution here is directed against two classes of people; the woman - probably representing believing Israel; and Gentile believers. The entire people of God become the object of the dragon's pursuit. Yet, in the midst of that persecution, the woman will be protected.

In verse six we are told the woman fled into the desert to a

112

place prepared for her by God that she might be taken care of for 1,260 days. In verses thirteen and fourteen we are told the woman was given "two wings of a great eagle" so that she might fly to the place prepared for her in the desert where she would be protected. During this period of persecution, God provides an escape. He prepares a place for the woman; he divinely protects his people. The "wings of an eagle" are a symbol throughout the Bible of God's faithfulness in caring for, and delivering his people.

Throughout history, behind the efforts to persecute and exterminate the people of God, there stands a dragon: Satan. But, in the midst of Satan's attacks, God is there.

CHAPTER SEVENTEEN: *The Antichrist*

And the dragon stood on the shore of the sea. And I saw a beast coming out of the sea, (Rev. 13:1).

At this point in *Revelation* John saw two images that symbolically represent the primary vehicles through which the dragon will pursue the woman during the end times. This chapter contains the vision of two beasts. One is a beast he saw coming out of the sea. The other came out of the earth.

The first beast symbolizes the antichrist and his empire. In the last days a man will appear who will be the incarnation of evil itself. In the same way that Jesus Christ is the incarnation of God in the flesh, the antichrist will be the incarnation of Satan in the flesh.

This person is referred to throughout the Bible by several names. John, in an earlier letter, called him the antichrist, (I Jn. 2:18). Paul called him the "man of lawlessness," (II Thess. 2:3). Jesus referred to him as the "one who causes desolation" – a reference to the same person identified to Daniel in his apocalyptic vision, (Daniel 9:27). This "beast" is the human archenemy of the people of God: thus, the "anti Christ".

The message concerning the beast in *Revelation* is rooted in the prophecies of the book of *Daniel*. In Daniel's day, Nebuchadnezzar, King of the Babylonian Empire, had a dream. The young Jewish captive Daniel interpreted the dream for Nebuchadnezzar. The dream involved a statue. This statue represented four world kingdoms that would appear on the stage of human history. The first world kingdom was represented by the head of gold. That head of gold represented Nebuchadnezzar and the Babylonian Empire.

After the head of gold, the statue had a chest and arms of silver. This part of the statue represented the coming Medo-Persian Empire. The statue's belly and thighs of bronze represented a third world empire that would conquer the Persians: the Greek. The fourth empire, represented by feet of iron and clay, would be the Roman Empire.

Daniel prophesied that this fourth empire would be a divided empire. During the second phase of this empire's reign, God's kingdom would be established on earth. The Kingdom of God would crush this world empire and be established as an eternal kingdom. This dream and interpretation were confirmed by a vision Daniel himself had. His vision is recorded in *Daniel* chapter seven.

Daniel had a vision of four beasts. The first beast was like a lion, the second like a bear, the third like a leopard, and the fourth was described as terrifying, frightening, and powerful. The coming of the Messiah, and the establishment of his kingdom, followed the appearance of the fourth beast.

This chapter in *Daniel* spans the entire period of world history from the time of ancient Babylon through the second coming of Jesus Christ. The angel who interpreted the dream told Daniel that these four beasts symbolized four great kingdoms. The ten horns of the final beast symbolized ten kings. One horn was seen waging war against the saints until the Son of Man came.

This "horn" appears again in *Daniel* chapter 9. This chapter contains the prophecy of the seventy weeks of *Daniel*. The seventieth week of Daniel's vision is often equated with the tribulation period of *Revelation*. Those final seven years revolve around a ruler that Gabriel told Daniel would come from the people who would destroy the city of Jerusalem. The "He" that is spoken of by Gabriel in *Daniel* is the beast that now comes up out of the sea here in *Revelation*.

The First Beast
The dragon gave the beast his power and his throne and great authority, (Rev. 13:2).

John saw a beast coming up out of the sea. The sea was often a symbol of the Gentile nations. This beast represented a coming world kingdom. The beast had ten horns and seven heads, with ten crowns on his horns, and on each head, a blasphemous name. The fourth beast of Daniel's vision had ten horns representing ten kings or kingdoms. The reduction to seven heads here alludes to the fact that out of the ten kingdoms, three will be usurped by one of the kings. This king will eventually rise to become the antichrist.

Revelation tells us that this kingdom will be satanically empowered. If we live in the end-times, we can begin to look for the development of a powerful empire with an incredibly charismatic leader.

We live in a time when there is a tremendous push toward world centralization. Humanists are pushing for a "new global order." Economists are advocating a centralization of the world's

116

monetary systems. Some politicians advocate centralization of power and one-world government. It won't happen on a worldwide basis. It will primarily take place among Western European nations that trace their origins to the old Roman Empire.

In the end-times the world will reach a breaking point. There will be economic chaos, runaway inflation, energy crisis, volatile political unrest, and a breakdown of sanity on a worldwide scale. As has often happened in human history, the stage will be set for a powerful personality to come along, promising peace and personal prosperity.

Without sounding paranoid, it is possible that behind the scenes, people of great power will actually generate and precipitate the crisis for the purpose of forcing us into the geopolitical scenario portrayed in *Revelation.*

Prophetically, this last world empire has a connection to the old Roman Empire. Rome fulfilled the prophecy of the destruction of Jerusalem. Rome was "the people of the ruler who will come." Rome was the great persecutor of the first century church as John wrote. Rome was the fourth world power.

I should point out that in the last three hundred years a view of *Revelation* has developed called the preterist view. Those who interpret *Revelation* through this grid believe that the entire book was fulfilled in the first century. Rome was the beast. Caesar was the antichrist. According to this view nothing about the book but the last few chapters is about the future. This certainly wasn't the understanding or approach of the first three hundred years of church history.

If this end-times power has its roots in the people, culture, and geography of the old Roman Empire then it will arise out of Western Europe and the United States. You can see why many biblical scholars have kept a very careful eye on the European Union, and organizations like the G8.

The most significant information contained in these verses is the response of the unbelieving world to the beast. We are told that the whole world will follow the beast and worship the dragon. Men will ask, "Who is like the beast? Who can make war against him?" (Rev. 13:40.)

The beast will wield tremendous political, military, and economic power that will give the world a false sense of peace and security. Paul wrote that when the whole world is saying "peace and safety," suddenly destruction would come upon them,

(I Thessalonians 5:3).

Consider this as a possible scenario: At the beginning of the seven-year countdown, the antichrist will surface as a man of peace. He will be viewed like a savior who will bring answers to a world in crisis. Halfway through this period, it will be as if Satan himself comes to indwell this person. He will blaspheme God, exalt himself, demand worship, and persecute the people of God.

The False Prophet

Then I saw another beast, coming out of the earth. He had two horns like a lamb, but he spoke like a dragon. He exercised all the authority of the first beast on his behalf, and made the earth and its inhabitants worship the first beast, whose fatal wound had been healed," (Rev. 13:11-12).

This second beast plays a significant role in the rise to power of the first. We have already seen that the first beast is a person who holds tremendous political, military and economic power. What we see in the second half of this chapter is a move towards spiritual centralization. This beast is the false prophet. He helps create an end-times "religion".

The religion that evolves at this time might take a form that we usually do not associate with "religion." For instance, the "religion" of the end times might be secular humanism. Properly understood, secular humanism elevates man to the position of God. It puts man at the center of the universe, and man worships himself.

Or, this end times "religion" might contain elements of communism or socialism where the state is elevated to the place of God. There appears to be within this "religion" elements of the occult and the supernatural.

Having abandoned the authority and spiritual foundations of the Judeo-Christian heritage, politicians, physicians, educators and theologians could advocate the merging of western technology and its power structures with eastern philosophy, mysticism, and the occult. Of course, it will be packaged in a way that will deceive the average man or woman who that doesn't have the biblical background to discern its error.

If you put all the possibilities together you would have a religion with elements of humanism, where man is worshipped; socialism, where the state is worshipped; Eastern philosophy where literally everything is worshipped; and occultism, where Satan is worshipped; all rolled into one big "religion."

The second beast is given the title "the False Prophet". The title, "false prophet" comes from a passage later in *Revelation* where we read:

Then I saw the beast and the kings of the earth and their armies gathered together to make war against the rider of the horse and his army. But the beast was captured and with him the false prophet who had performed the miraculous signs on his behalf. With these signs he had deluded those who had received the mark of the beast and worshipped his image. The two of them were thrown alive into the fiery lake of burning sulphur, (Rev. 19:19-20).

The false prophet is the spiritual leader of the antichrist. In the same way that the Holy Spirit leads a person to commitment to and worship of Jesus Christ, the false prophets will eventually lead people to worship and commit themselves to the antichrist.

This second beast looks like a lamb, but speaks like a dragon. Outwardly, he will look religious, but inwardly he will be demonic. He will be the greatest master of demonic deception the world has ever known. He will have the ability to perform supernatural and miraculous signs. The fact that he comes out of the earth infers that this person might actually arise out of Israel.

We live in a time where we are seeing a resurgence of the supernatural. We need to be aware that the Holy Spirit is not the only spirit that is in the business of producing supernatural and miraculous phenomena. In the end times, people will be deceived by demonic supernatural phenomena. Paul warned the Christians in Thessalonica:

The coming of the lawless one will be in accordance with the work of Satan displayed in all kinds of counterfeit miracles, signs and wonders, and in every sort of evil that deceives those who are perishing. They perish because they refused to love the truth and so to be saved, (II Thess. 2:9).

The false prophet also sets up an image and commands people to worship this image. This image in *Revelation* is probably what Daniel and Jesus referred to as the "abomination of desolation," (Daniel 9:27, Matt. 24:15).

The terminology that is used to describe this event, "the abomination of desolation," historically has its roots in Israel's history. Around 170 B.C. the Seluecid ruler Antiochus Epiphanes set out to Hellenize Israel. He gave himself the name "Epiphanes" which means "god manifest." The Jews in derision called him "Epimanes," which means "madman." He attempted to force Greek customs on the Jews. After facing stiff resistance, he captured Jerusalem, executed 80,000 Jews, and made circumcision and possession of the Torah offenses punishable by death. He entered the Holy Place of the temple, and in that Holy Place erected an altar to Zeus. On that altar to Zeus, he sacrificed a pig. The Jews refer to that historic event as "the abomination of desolation."

In 165 B.C., the Jews under the leadership of the Judas Maccabeus overthrew Antiochus. The temple was cleansed and rededicated. The Jews still celebrate this event at Hanukkah: the Festival of Lights.

Antiochus serves as a type of antichrist. In the same way Antiochus desecrated the Temple in his time, the antichrist will desecrate the Temple (literal or symbolic) in the end times. Antiochus also corrupted the Jewish priesthood by removing the authentic Jewish High Priest, Jason, and putting into power his own man, Menalaus. Menalaus tried to encourage the Jewish people to Hellenize and to worship Antiochus. Antiochus and Menalaus provide a historical conception of how the antichrist and the false prophet will operate. The false prophet draws the whole world away from the worship of the true God into worship of the antichrist.

The important message of this particular passage is a message about consequences. People will either give their allegiance to the antichrist, or they will die:

He was given power to give breath to the image of the first beast so that it could speak and cause all who refused to worship the image to be killed, (Rev. 13:15).

This was exactly what was happening in John's day. In the letters to the churches we saw that many believers were put to death because they refused to worship Caesar. The same kind of a situation is going to develop in the end-times. Earlier in the chapter we read:

120

All inhabitants of the earth will worship the beast, all whose names have not been written in the book of life, belonging to the Lamb that was slain from the creation of the world, (Rev. 13:8).

A very important polarization is taking place at this point in *Revelation.* On the one hand there are those who worship the beast. Their names are not written in the book of the Lamb. They have no personal commitment to Jesus Christ. When you make a personal commitment to Jesus Christ, and receive him as Lord and Savior, your name is written in the Lamb's Book of Life. Those who do not receive Jesus Christ do not have their names written in the Lamb's Book of Life. On the other hand, many are so committed to Jesus Christ that they are willing to die for their faith.

One of the main characteristics of the tribulation period is that it will be a time when a clear choice will have to be made. People will either be committed to Jesus Christ or to Antichrist. There will be no easy decisions during this time. It will be black or white.

The Cost of Commitment

Those who worship Jesus will face the same consequences for their choice as the believers in John's day. Throughout *Revelation* we have seen this message clearly. Remember these earlier texts:

He who has an ear, let him hear...If anyone is to be killed with the sword, with the sword he will be killed. This calls for patient endurance and faithfulness on the part of the saints, (Rev. 13:9-10).

They overcame him by the blood of the Lamb and by the word of their testimony; they did not love their lives so much as to shrink from death, (Rev. 12:11).

Now when they have finished their testimony, the beast that comes up from the Abyss will attack them, and overpower and kill them, (Rev. 11:7).

These are they who have come out of the great tribulation; they have washed their robes and made them white in the blood of the Lamb, (Rev. 7:14).

Then each of them was given a white robe, and they were told to wait a little longer, until the number of fellow servants and brothers who were to be killed as they had been was completed, (Rev. 6:11).

I know where you live, where Satan has his throne. Yet you remain true to my name. You did not renounce your faith in me, even in the days of Antipas, my faithful witness, who was put to death in your city, where Satan lives, (Rev. 2:13).

Do not be afraid of what you are about to suffer. I tell you, the devil will put some of you in prison to test you and you will suffer persecution for ten days. Be faithful even to the point of death, and I will give you the crown of life, (Rev. 2:10).

I, John, your brother and companion in the suffering and kingdom and patient endurance that are ours in Jesus, was on the island of Patmos because of the word of God and the testimony of Jesus, (Rev. 1:9).

The message to the believer throughout *Revelation* is that genuine faith is costly. From John's day till the end of the age a costly choice must be made. The ultimate question for every human being is, "Whose mark will I bear? The mark of the beast, or the seal of the living God?"

The Mark of the Beast
He also forced everyone...to receive a mark, (Rev. 13:16).

John tells us that the beast forced people, regardless of whether they are important or insignificant, rich or poor, free or slave to receive a mark on their hands or foreheads. The word translated "mark" here is the Greek word *charagma*. The word had several uses in John's day.

The *charagma* was a sign of ownership. In the Roman army a *charagma* was a mark signifying devotion to a specific general. It spoke of submission to authority. It was also the word used to identify the certificate of worship received when a Roman citizen burned his pinch of incense to Caesar. To receive the mark of the beast demonstrates that a choice has been made to worship and submit to the antichrist.

By the second century of church history, the church fathers were no longer sure what this "mark" was. I think we need to be aware that we cannot be absolutely certain either! Much of our interpretation of Revelation requires a ealthy bit of humility.

John also tells us that this mark is either the name or number of the beast. He identifies the number of the beast as 666. Throughout church history people have had a tremendous tendency to perform numerical gymnastics with the number.

In both Hebrew and Greek, letters serve as numbers. Most of us are familiar with Roman numerals. Roman numerals are Latin letters that are being used as numbers. Consequently, words have numerical equivalents. People have used these numbers in different ways to come up with an amazing variety of interpretations concerning the name of the antichrist. The early church came up with a variety of options.

The word *latinas* had the numeral equivalent of 666. It was a word that represented the Roman Empire. Therefore, to take the mark of the beast was to pledge allegiance to the Roman Empire.

Titan was the family name of the Roman emperors Titus, Vespasian, and Domitian. If you add the numerical value of that name in a certain way, it has a numerical equivalent of 666. The Greek word *arnoumai* means, "I deny". There is a way to give this word the same numerical equivalent. Therefore, to deny that Jesus was Lord, and to confess that Caesar was Lord, was to receive the mark.

In Latin, the word *Neron*, which is the name of Caesar Nero, could be given the same numerical equivalent. In Hebrew, the name Nero Caesar could also have the numerical equivalent of 666. This led to the early belief that antichrist would be Nero resurrected. All these options were dogmatically identified as the "true" meaning of 666.

During the Reformation, the reformers identified the Pope as the antichrist. They had ways of figuring how the word "Pope" could add up to 666. The Catholic church responded by accusing the reformers of being the antichrist and had ways of calculating how "John Calvin" and "Martin Luther" could add up to 666. Later, Napoleon was identified as the antichrist. During World War II it was Hitler. In our day, I have heard everyone from Henry Kissinger to Anwar Sadat to George Bush to Barak Obama identified as the antichrist.

What is the significance of the number identified as the mark of the beast? Six is the number of man; three is the number of God. 666 symbolizes a man making himself God. That is exactly what the antichrist will do! When a person pledges allegiance to antichrist's system, he will instantly become a "marked man."

Receiving the mark of the beast will involve making a conscious choice both to worship the beast and to receive his mark. There are significant consequences of either taking this mark, or not taking it.

What if you do not take the mark? John tells us, "No one could buy or sell, unless he had the mark, which is the name of the beast or the number of his name," (Rev. 13:16). The antichrist will wield such economic power and control that if a person refuses to give allegiance to him, they will be unable to buy or sell in the marketplace. Believers will be forced to go underground as they did in the first three centuries of church history. Ultimately, believers will face martyrdom for refusing to take the mark. They will be viewed as political traitors who are unwilling to pledge allegiance to the one person who can supposedly bring peace to the world. On the other hand, there is a good consequence to not taking the mark of the beast:

I saw thrones on which were seated those who had been given authority to judge. And I saw the souls of those who had been beheaded because of their testimony for Jesus and because of the word of God. They had not worshipped the beast or his image and had not received his mark on their foreheads are on their hands. They came to life and reigned with Christ 1,000 years, (Rev. 20:5-6).

At first glance it appears that there are serious consequences to not receiving the mark of the beast. In reality, there are more serious consequences to receiving the mark. John will go on to write:

If anyone worships the beast and his image and receives his mark on the forehead or on the hand, he too, will drink of the wine of God's fury, which has been poured full strength into the cup of his wrath. He will be tormented with burning sulphur in the presence of the holy angels and of the Lamb. And the smoke of their torment rises for ever and ever. There is no rest, day or night, for those who worship the beast and his image, or for anyone who receives the mark of his name, (Rev. 14:9-11).

This message is followed by a warning:

This calls for patient endurance on the part of the saints who obey God's commandments and remain faithful to Jesus, (Rev. 14:12).

The consequences of receiving the mark are much greater than the consequences of not receiving it.

Marked Men

Then I looked, and there before me was the Lamb, standing on Mt. Zion, and with him 144,000 who had his name and his Father's name written on their foreheads, (Rev. 14:1).

Immediately following the description of the mark of the beast, John had a vision of a different kind of "marked" man. John saw a hundred forty-four thousand men who had God's name written on their foreheads rather than bearing the mark of the beast. The message of chapters thirteen through the first part of chapter fourteen is that everyone, ultimately, bears one of two marks. You either stand with the beast or you stand with the Lamb.

This Mt. Zion is not in Jerusalem. This is the heavenly Mt. Zion, (Heb. 12:22). These hundred forty-four thousand bear Christ's mark of ownership. They sing before God's throne. They are called "the redeemed of the earth," (Rev. 14:3). John says they are undefiled.

This passage is not talking about a hundred forty-four thousand Jewish boys who have never had a sexual experience. It is talking about those that have not defiled themselves spiritually. To worship the beast, to receive his mark, is to commit spiritual adultery. The Holy Spirit again communicates a message to the church of John's day that is also a message to the church in our day. The message tells us to be patient; be willing to suffer; resist the forces of evil; reject the mark of the beast; make sure you are marked with the seal of the living God.

CHAPTER EIGHTEEN: *The Grapes of Wrath*

I looked, and there before me was a white cloud, and seated on the cloud was one 'like a son of man' with a crown of gold on his head and a sharp sickle in his hand...The angel swung his sickle on the earth, gathered its grapes and threw them into the great winepress of God's wrath, (Rev. 14:14,19).

We now come to the place in *Revelation* where God's wrath is expressed in judgment. There are two Greek words that are translated "wrath" in the New Testament. One is the Greek word *thumos*, which is sometimes translated "anger." The other is the Greek word *orge.* Usually, when the New Testament speaks of God's wrath, it uses the word *orge.* This passage consistently talks about the *thumos*, or the anger of God.

God's nature consists of a variety of attributes. Love is one of the essential elements of God's nature. God's love is expressed in His acts of grace and mercy. But God has not only revealed himself as a God of love, but also as a God of righteousness and justice.

Righteousness and justice are said to be the foundations of His throne, (Ps. 97:2). This righteous dimension of God's nature is expressed in the judgment of sin. Just as God must love, he must also be righteous. God's love is never expressed apart from his righteousness, and God's righteousness is never expressed apart from his love.

If we do not have an understanding of the balance of these two attributes we will either have a view of God as a sentimental God who can overlook sin and evil, pat us on the back, and be our big buddy in the sky; or we are going to have a view of God as some kind of ogre who delights in tossing sinners into Hell. Love and righteousness are both dimensions of God's character. We will see how the two work together in a minute.

Grace and Wrath

We live in an age of grace. God is a God of grace and mercy. In the Old Testament, we see much of God's righteous anger expressed in judgment. But even the Old Testament is filled with examples of the grace and mercy of God.

At Mt. Sinai, God gave Israel his law, (Ex. 19:1- 20:17). The Law was an expression of God's righteousness. But immediately after giving the Law, God gave the Israelites the plans for the Tabernacle. The Tabernacle was an expression of God's grace. The Law set the standard Israel was expected to live up to. The Tabernacle was a place of forgiveness. In a sense God was saying, "I know you are not going to meet the demands of the Law, so I will provide a means whereby your failure can be forgiven." The Tabernacle was a gift from a God of grace.

In the New Testament, these dimensions of God's nature are expressed perfectly in Jesus Christ. Through Christ, God provided a way for his love to be expressed while at the same time his righteousness was not compromised. The cross is the fullest expression of this balance of love and righteousness.

If God were just a God of sentimental love, not righteous love, Christ would not have had to die on the cross. The cross was the place where God's just demands were met. He executed judgment on the sin of the world by the death of his own son, Jesus Christ. When we receive the free gift of salvation in Jesus Christ, our sins have not just been passed over as if God has said, "No big deal." Our sins have been judged at the cross of Jesus Christ. God can now demonstrate total love and grace toward us, because in Christ his justice and righteousness have been satisfied. God only requires one condition. We must be willing to receive the gift of salvation. Salvation means "deliverance from destruction." The judgment that now takes place in *Revelation* is God's righteous judgment executed upon a world that has rejected the gift of grace he has offered in Jesus Christ.

The Heavenly Temple

After this I looked, and I saw in heaven the temple—that is, the tabernacle of the covenant law—and it was opened. Out of the temple came the seven angels with the seven plagues. They were dressed in clean, shining linen and wore golden sashes around their chests. Then one of the four living creatures gave to the seven angels seven golden bowls filled with the wrath of God, who lives for ever and ever. And the temple was filled with smoke from the glory of God and from his power, and no one could enter the temple until the seven plagues of the seven angels were completed, (Rev. 15:5-8).

The final judgment of God originates from the temple in heaven. The temple in heaven is a picture of the dwelling place of God.

When Moses was given instructions for building the tabernacle, he was told to build it exactly according to the pattern God gave him. In *Hebrews*, we are told the reason for this instruction was that the earthly tabernacle was to be a copy of the true heavenly temple, (Heb. 8:5). John now sees this true temple.

The earthly tabernacle and temple were divided into several spaces. There was a specific Greek word (*naos*) that referred to the sanctuary or Holy Place inside the Temple complex. That Greek word is used consistently throughout this passage. The Holy Place, or sanctuary, was further divided into two rooms. The room where the Ark of the Covenant was kept was called the Holy of Holies. Inside the Ark were the tablets of the Law delivered to Moses on Mt. Sinai. Two golden cherubim hovered over the Ark of the Covenant, representing the righteousness of God.

Between the cherubim, over the Ark of the Covenant, God manifested His *shekinah* glory. On top of the Ark of the Covenant was a covering called the mercy seat or place of atonement. It was there, on the mercy seat, that once a year the high priest would sprinkle the blood of a sacrifice to atone for, or cover, the sins of the people of Israel.

All this foreshadowed the sacrifice of Jesus Christ. The book of *Hebrews* tells us that Jesus Christ went into the real tabernacle in Heaven, and there in the presence of God, at the heavenly mercy seat, sprinkled his own blood as a sin offering, once and for all, (Heb. 9:11-12). By God's grace, those who accept that sin offering as atonement for their sin are delivered from the judgment of God. It is significant to recognize that it is from this same heavenly Holy Place that judgment now proceeds. This is judgment destined only for those who have rejected the free gift of God's grace. All that has not been "covered" by the blood of Christ is now subject to the wrath of God.

The Bowls of Wrath

The outpouring of the seven bowls of God's wrath completes God's judgment. There is a sequence in the three sets of judgments in *Revelation*. The seal judgments contained a partial judgment. The trumpet judgments contained a more severe judgment. This outpouring of the bowls of wrath ends in total cataclysmic destruction. That which was only partial in the seal and trumpet judgments becomes complete with the outpouring of the bowls.

*The first angel went and poured out his bowl on the land, and ugly
and painful sores broke out on the people who had the mark of the
beast and worshipped his image,* (Rev 16:2).

The first bowl is related to the fifth trumpet. Both involve
pain and suffering inflicted on those who are "marked." The fifth
trumpet is directed toward those who do not have "the seal of God
on their foreheads," while the first bowl is directed toward those
"who had the mark of the beast."

*The second angel poured out his bowl on the sea, and it turned
into blood like that of a dead man, and every living thing in the sea
died,* (Rev 16:3).

The second bowl is definitely related to the second trumpet.
The trumpet judgment turned one-third of the sea into blood,
resulting in the death of one-third of the living creatures of the sea.
The bowl judgment results in all of the sea being turned to blood
and every living thing in the sea dying. We are not told the "how"
of the judgment, only the results.

*The third angel poured out his bowl on the rivers and springs of
water, and they became blood,* (Rev. 16:4).

The third bowl is directly related to the third trumpet. Both
judgments affect the rivers and springs of the world. Again, the
trumpet judgment resulted in a partial destruction of these fresh
water sources while the results of the bowl judgment are total.
Again, we are not told the "how" of the bowl judgment, but here
we do receive a "why":

*Then I heard the angel in charge of the waters say: 'You are just
in these judgments, you who are and who were, the Holy One,
because you have so judged; for they have shed the blood of your
saints and prophets, and you have given them blood to drink as
they deserve,'* (Rev. 16:5,6).

The fourth bowl is preceded by the declaration, "Yes, Lord
God Almighty, true and just are your judgments." This declaration
is followed by the action of the fourth bowl:

The fourth angel poured out his bowl on the sun, and the sun was given power to scorch people with fire. They were seared by the intense heat and they cursed the name of God, who had control over these plagues, but they refused to repent and glorify him, (Rev. 16:8-9).

The judgment of this bowl is scorching heat from the sun. It is obvious that those affected by this judgment recognize its source. But look at their response. They curse God and refuse to repent. By this point, the people of the world have become so warped by their relationship with the beast that they are spiritually unsalvageable. Judgment continues:

The fifth angel poured out his bowl on the throne of the beast, and his kingdom was plunged into darkness. Men gnawed their tongues in agony and cursed the God of heaven because of their pains and their sores, but they refused to repent of what they had done, (Rev 16:10-11).

The fifth bowl is related to the fourth trumpet. The trumpet produced a one-third reduction of the light of the sun while the bowl casts the entire kingdom of the beast into total darkness.

The sixth angel poured out his bowl on the great river Euphrates, and its water was dried up to prepare the way for the kings from the East, (Rev.16:12).

There is a strong possibility that the source of destruction of the bowls and trumpets is connected with the Battle of Armageddon. When the sixth trumpet sounded, we were introduced to a military force of two hundred million troops at the river Euphrates. The sixth bowl identifies these troops as the "kings from the East."

Along with these forces, we are told that demonic forces will gather "the kings of the whole world" to a placed called Armageddon to engage in "the battle of the great day of God Almighty." We will look at this battle in more detail in a minute.

The seventh angel poured out his bowl into the air, and out of the temple came a loud voice from the throne, saying, 'It is done!' (Rev. 16:17)

The outpouring of the seventh bowl takes us back to the opening of the sixth seal. Both of these judgments involve earthquakes of such a magnitude that mountains, islands and cities are leveled. The phrase "ultimate cosmic cataclysm" might describe the outcome of the final bowl.

Part of the outpouring of this final bowl involves the destruction of "Babylon the Great." We will examine Babylon in more detail in the next chapter, but here we should note that the events of the next two chapters of Revelation fall under the umbrella of the outpouring of the seventh bowl.

Three events are grouped together at the end of the tribulation period: the battle of Armageddon; the destruction of Babylon the Great; and the second coming of Jesus Christ. For the present, let us turn our attention to the first event in this sequence.

Armageddon

At the Battle of Armageddon, the nations of the world converge on the Holy Land and enter into the final battle of history. We get the impression from what Jesus said that if He did not intervene in this battle, mankind would annihilate itself, (Mt. 24:22). With the current nuclear capabilities of the major world powers, mankind has within its grasp the ability to destroy itself. Jesus Christ is the one who will keep that from happening.

We are told that the place where this battle is going to be fought is called Armageddon. Har is the Hebrew word for "mountain," "Megeddon" refers to Megiddo, a town in northern Israel. Armageddon literally means "the mountain of Megiddo." Spanning the center of this region of northern Israel is a large, open plain called the Valley of Jezreel. This particular area has been a significant battlefield throughout Israel's history.

In the Old Testament, it was here on the plains of Megiddo that Deborah and Barak overthrew Sisera, (Judges chapters 4 and 5). This was the place where Jehu defeated Joram and Ahaziah, (II Kings 9). It was also the place where Josiah was killed by Pharoah Neco, (II Kings 23:29). Napoleon, looking over this valley, said it was the ideal battlefield on which to gather the armies of the world to engage in battle. This will be the place where the final battle of history takes place.

Prophetically, we know that in the end-times there will be five major spheres of power in the world. The first sphere will be Israel itself. This is significant, since from 70 A.D. until 1948, Israel did not exist as a nation. The rebirth of the nation of Israel is central to the prophetic picture.

Daniel and *Ezekiel* both referred to blocks of power that Daniel called "the Kings of the North" and "the Kings of the South," (Daniel 11:40). Ezekiel's prophecy identified this southern coalition as consisting of Persia (modern Iran and Iraq), Cush (modern Ethiopia), and Put (modern Libya).

The modern nations occupying these ancient lands are all Muslim nations, hostile to Israel. *Ezekiel* identified the northern coalition with the following description:

Son of man, set your face against Gog, of the land of Magog, the prince of Rosh, Meshech, and Tubal, (Ez. 38:2).

There is good evidence to support the theory that this nation to the "uttermost north" of Israel, and the tribes spoken of, are the ancient forefathers of modern Russia.

The fourth sphere of power is the ten-nation confederacy with roots in the old Roman Empire. This is the power from which antichrist will arise.

The fifth sphere of power is called the "kings of the East" and consists of a military force of two hundred million troops. This force comes from east of the Euphrates. The options of what modern nations could be identified with the kings of the East include Iran, India, China, and Japan.

A close look at the prevailing blocks of political power in the world today, compared with the prophetic pictures of *Daniel*, *Ezekiel*, and *Revelation* presents us with some very interesting "coincidences." Is it any wonder that this scenario, coupled with the staggering problems of the world today, have caused many students of Bible prophecy to project that we are nearing the end years of world history and heading full-steam toward Armageddon? Putting the pieces of the prophetic puzzle together, we might come up with a speculative scenario that looks something like this:

Russia and Syria attack Israel from the north. Iran and the countries of the Arab Spring join the attack from the south. We need to remember that many of these Arab nations are dedicated to the annihilation of Israel as a Jewish state.

Ezekiel prophesied that when the Kings of the North make their move, and attack Israel, they will be totally annihilated. The northern power will be virtually wiped off the face of the earth.

Ezekiel says that it will take seven months to bury the dead, (Ezekiel 39:12). For seven years Israel will be partially fueled by the leftover implements of that war, (Ezekiel 39:9). The destruction of the northern power will pave the way for the eastern power to make its move. As they mobilize and head west from the Euphrates, the western power, headed by the as yet unidentified antichrist, prepares to come to Israel's aid. Prior to these battles, a treaty has been made between Israel and the west that launched the seven-year period of the Tribulation. At the three-and-a-half-year mark, things changed. The antichrist's true colors have started to show.

The western alliance moves into Israel and establishes their base in the Valley of Jezreel, opposite *Har Meggido*. The eastern armies and the western armies engage in combat. It is a terribly bloody conflict, and the west defeats the east.

Then, the antichrist betrays his treaty with Israel and turns his forces and heads toward Jerusalem. When this happens, Zechariah prophesied that the remaining nations of the earth will align themselves against Israel, (Zech. 12-14). With the antichrist and his forces surrounding Jerusalem, and the world on the brink of destruction, Jesus Christ returns, (Zechariah 14:4-5; Revelation 19:11-21). The armies of heaven destroy the antichrist and his forces. This scenario is purely speculative, but it gives you some idea of how the pieces could easily fit together in our times.

When this chapter comes to a close, the second coming of Christ is near. Perhaps the most significant message of the chapter is not what God does, but how men respond to what God does. Three times in the chapter, we are told that those affected by these judgments curse God, (Rev. 16:9,11,21). Twice we are told that they refuse to repent (Rev. 16: 9,11). God's judgment is vindicated by the response of those He judges. "Babylon" is beyond repentance; God's grace has reached its limits. When those two realities collide, the angels come forth from the temple and the bowls of wrath are poured out. The end is near.

CHAPTER NINETEEN: *The Fall of Babylon*

One of the seven angels who had the seven bowls came and said to me, "Come, I will show you the punishment of the great prostitute, who sits by many waters, (Rev. 17:1).

Babylon

Earlier in *Revelation* John heard an angel declare, "Fallen! Fallen is Babylon the Great," (Rev. 14:8). The fulfillment of that proclamation is found here in the next two chapters of *Revelation*. To understand the message of the angel, and what happens at this point in John's vision, we need to identify what "Babylon" refers to.

Babylon first appears in the Bible in *Genesis*. In what is called the Table of nations, we are told:

Cush was the father of Nimrod, who grew to be a mighty warrior on the earth. He was a mighty hunter before the Lord; that is why it is said, 'Like Nimrod, a mighty hunter before the Lord.' The first centers of his kingdom were Babylon, Erech, Accad and Calneh in Shinar, (Genesis 10:8-10).

Babylon was part of the kingdom ruled by a man named Nimrod. The name of the city is connected to the building of the Tower of Babel. It has been suggested that the word *babel* had its origins in the word *bab-eli*, meaning "the gate of God". The above reference in *Genesis* hints that building the tower was Nimrod's idea.

Nimrod's name means "rebel," or "we will revolt." At the site of ancient Babylon, Nimrod gathered together a group of men to build a monument. In *Genesis* we read an invitation to rebellion quite possibly spoken by Nimrod:

Come, let us build ourselves a city, with a tower that reaches to the heavens, so that we may make a name for ourselves and not be scattered over the face of the whole earth, (Rev. 12:4).

Note the phrase, "that we may make a name for ourselves." This tower was an attempt to elevate the importance of man to the place that only God was to occupy. It also was a monument to rebellion against God's intention of humanity spreading out and populating the entire planet. Rather than scattering over the whole earth, Nimrod and his cohorts decided to centralize and build this tower. The result was chaos and confusion.

Rather than becoming the gate to God, and a monument to human ego, the place became Babel, a word meaning "confusion". Whenever people seek to usurp the place that only God rightfully occupies, the result is always confusion. In its very origins, Babylon was a city where people rebelled against God's authority.

By Daniel's day, the city of Babylon was the capital of a major world empire. This was the city where the captives were taken when the Babylonians destroyed the kingdom of Judah and carried into captivity the finest young men of Israel. The book of *Daniel* was written from Babylon.

Astrology, sorcery, and spiritualism were all part of the Babylonian mystery religions of Daniel's day. Those religions infiltrated almost every area of the known world. To a Jew, "Babylon" represented the attempt of men to usurp God's authority, a man-made pseudo-religion, and a lifestyle that was abominable to God.

When John wrote about "Babylon the Great," his reader would have all these images flowing through his mind. If there is any one concept which "Babylon" symbolizes in *Revelation*, it would be what the Bible calls "the world." Babylon is godless society--the world system. There is no doubt that when John wrote *Revelation* he saw Rome, the power of Rome, and all that Rome stood for, as "Babylon." Our challenge is to see beyond the first century application of the symbol to the end-times fulfillment of what *Revelation* calls "Babylon the Great."

Three Greek words are constantly repeated when Babylon is referred to in these chapters. The first is the Greek word *porne*. The second is the Greek word *porneuo*, which is the verb form of the first word, and the third is the Greek word *porneia*. The first word, *porne*, means "a whore, an adulteress or a prostitute." The second word, *porneuo*, is a verb that means "to commit adultery" or "to commit sexual immorality". The third word, *porneia*, is a noun identifying the actual act of immorality, fornication, or adultery. Our word pornography is derived from these words.

All three of these words are used in the first two verses of this chapter in *Revelation*:

One of the seven angels who had the seven bowls came and

said to me, 'Come, I will show you the punishment of the great prostitute (porne) who sits on many waters. With her the kings of the earth committed adultery (porneuo) and the inhabitants of the earth were intoxicated with the wine of her adulteries (porneia),' (Rev. 17:1,2).

The concept of immorality is constantly associated with Babylon. John is probably not speaking of literal immorality. Adultery and immorality were always used symbolically to speak of Israel's unfaithfulness to God. Whenever Israel turned away from *YHWH,* and engaged in worship of the gods of the nations, she was accused of committing spiritual adultery.

In the book of *Hosea* we see how God viewed Israel as his own wife. The metaphor of the church as the bride of Christ is rooted in this Old Testament concept. God said that Israel was an adulteress who was "guilty of the vilest adultery in departing from the Lord," (Hosea 1:2). He went on to declare, "A spirit of prostitution is in their heart; they do not acknowledge the Lord," (Hosea 5:4). When the Christian of John's day would read about Babylon, the whore, he would think immediately of the world system and the power that system has to seduce men and women away from a commitment to Christ.

Babylon, the whore, has a repertoire of devices with which she seduces people. She uses materialism. We will see in these chapters that the kings and the merchants of earth weep and mourn over the destruction of Babylon because all of the world's economic systems have been destroyed.

She uses spiritualism. She seduces people away from a worship of God by deceiving them with a variety of spiritual experiences. She uses religion. She seduces people through religion so that they become self-righteous and do not sense their need of salvation. She uses immorality.

Babylon employs anything that is able to seduce men and women away from Jesus. In *Revelation* she is dressed in purple and scarlet and adorned with gold, precious stones and pearls. The finest things the world has to offer are available to the whore for the purposes of seduction. Her seduction is great, and we all face it daily!

The Whore and the Beast
This chapter reemphasizes the role of the beast, particularly in

relationship to the world system. John sees Babylon the Whore seated on the beast. One of the primary functions of the Anti-Christ system will be to promote the ideologies of the "Whore" called "Babylon." John is given more detailed instruction concerning the beast by one of the seven angels who poured out the bowls of wrath:

The seven heads are seven hills on which the woman sits. They are also seven kings. Five have fallen, one is, the other has not yet come; but when he does come, he must remain for a little while. The beast who once was, and now is not, is an eighth king. He belongs to the seven and is going to destruction, (Rev. 17:9-11).

I would be lying if I said this was easy material to interpret. If the kings referred to are actual kings then we can put together a scenario that fits this text. John was writing during the reign of Domitian. Five major emperors preceded Domitian; therefore, "five have fallen," Domitian would be referred to by the phrase "one is," and the future leader of the revived Roman Empire would be "the one who is yet to come."

Another possibility is that rather than referring to literal kings, this passage refers to kingdoms. Remember that Daniel's prophecy spoke of four world empires. The first was the Babylonian empire, followed by the Persian empire, followed by the Greek empire, and finally by the Roman empire. In Daniel's prophecy, the Roman empire would be revived in the end days and become the vehicle of Antichrist. Prior to the Babylonian empire, there were two other world empires. Both the Egyptian empire and the Assyrian empire preceded the Babylonian empire. If we plug those two empires into the formula, we then have seven world kingdoms. Five have fallen--Egypt, Assyria, Babylon, Persia, Greece; one is--Rome. One has not yet come --Revived Rome. The antichrist will arise out of that final kingdom. The beast would be an eighth kingdom growing out of the seventh kingdom; i.e., a revived Rome. Notice the way the purposes of the beast and its allies are described in verses 12-14:

The ten horns you saw are ten kings who have not yet received a kingdom, but who for one hour will receive authority as kings along with the beast. They have one purpose and will give their power and authority to the beast. They will make war against the Lamb,

138

*but the Lamb will overcome them because he is Lord of lords and
King of kings--and with him will be his called, chosen and faithful
followers,* (Revelation 17:12-14).

Also notice how John describes those who will be with Jesus
Christ when he returns. He gives them three credentials: they are
called, chosen, and faithful. Jesus Christ once said, "Many are
called, but few are chosen," (Matthew 22:14). The call goes out to
all men. The call involves the invitation to come into a relationship
with Christ. But few are chosen. Few respond to the invitation.
Those who respond are chosen and drawn into a relationship
with Christ. The "called" and "chosen" represent all those who
possess a relationship with Christ. But John also designates these
believers as "faithful." If many are called, but few are chosen,
fewer yet remain faithful. Again, this is one of the main messages
of *Revelation*. It is a call to believers to be faithful to Jesus.
Babylon represents the entire godless world system. Some
interpreters of *Revelation* focus on the religious dimension of
Babylon and say that Babylon the Great is an end-times religious
system. They believe it is a religious system that surfaces as a
support system of the beast. According to this view, Babylon is
related to the false prophet of *Revelation* chapter thirteen. They
would interpret this passage as relating to the way the antichrist
will use this end-times world religion to support him until he
achieves power.
But, if Babylon represents the entire godless world system,
then the message given here is significantly different. Antichrist
and his forces will destroy society as we know it. The beast will use
the structures of society until it rises to its position of prominence.
Then it will impose its own system on the world. Ironically, the
beast is the ultimate product of the godless world system. The
beast rules the City of Man! But in *Revelation,* it is the beast that
destroys the City of Man! Here is the paradox of the world system.
It carries within itself the seeds of its own destruction.

The Fall of Babylon
*'Fallen! Fallen is Babylon the Great!'...Then I heard another voice
from heaven say: 'Come out of her, my people, so that you will not
share in her sins, so that you will not receive any of her plagues,'*
(Rev. 18:1-2,4).

The message here is two-fold: 1) Babylon will be destroyed, and 2) God's people are to come out of "Babylon". Coming out of Babylon does not mean we reject people who do not believe. It also is not a command to reject God's creation. It is a challenge to us to make the decision to reject the ideology that the Bible calls "the world." John had written the same message to the same churches in his first letter:

Do not love the world or anything in the world. For everything in the world--the lust of the flesh, the lust of the eyes, and the pride of life--comes not from the Father but from the world. The world and its desires pass away, but the man who does the will of God lives forever, (I Jn. 2:15-17).

Every day, you and I are confronted with "Babylon". Every day, there are choices to be made. If we choose the world; we become spiritually unfaithful. If we choose Jesus, we will remain faithful to him.

With the message of the fall of Babylon, John is told how certain people will respond:

Response #1:

When the kings of the earth, who committed adultery with her and shared her luxury, see the smoke of her burning, they will weep and mourn over her. Terrified at her torment, they will stand far off and cry: 'Woe, Woe! O great city, O Babylon, city of power! In one hour your doom has come!' (Rev. 18:9-10).

The kings of the earth weep and mourn because suddenly they realize that their source of security is gone. They bet on the wrong horse! Babylon has been annihilated! We are told repeatedly that Babylon is destroyed in one hour. All throughout fallen human history we have had a world system constantly opposing the will of God. God has tolerated this opposition for his own purposes. But when the planned time comes, God acts, and in a flash, it is all gone!

Response #2:

The merchants of the earth will weep and mourn over her because

140

no one buys their cargoes any more-- cargoes of gold, silver, precious stones and pearls; fine linen, purple, silk and scarlet cloth; every sort of citron wood, and articles of every kind made of ivory, costly wood, bronze, iron and marble; cargoes of cinnamon and spice, of incense, myrrh and frankincense, of wine and olive oil, of fine flour and wheat; cattle and sheep; horses and carriages; and bodies and souls of men, (Rev. 18:11-13).

The businessmen of the world are devastated over the destruction of Babylon. Here is everything the world has to offer-- all these things the merchants of the earth have given their lives to pursue, rather than serving God. In the final chapter of *Revelation* John will see the New Jerusalem. Do you know what gold, silver and pearls are used for there? Construction materials! Gold is like tar; the streets are paved with it. All the world has to offer is nothing compared to what God has planned for those who seek him and not the world!

Response #3:

Every sea captain, and all who travel by ship, the sailors, and all who earn their living from the sea, will stand far off. When they see the smoke of her burning, they will exclaim, 'Was there ever a city like this great city?' They will throw dust on their heads, and with weeping and mourning cry out: 'Woe! Woe, O great city where all who had ships on the sea became rich through her wealth! In one hour she has been brought to ruin!' (Rev.18:17-19).

Three times we see the weeping and mourning of those who have committed their lives to the value system of Babylon. Now, all is lost. The end has come. Despair and destruction permeate their responses. But, there is an alternative.

Response #4:

Rejoice over her, O heaven! Rejoice, saints and apostles and prophets! God has judged her on the way she treated you, (Rev. 18:20).

There is one group of men and women who do not weep over Babylon. Their response is one of rejoicing. They have heeded the call of heaven and have "come out of her." Their citizenship is in heaven. Throughout history they have been persecuted and mistreated by Babylon. But now, Babylon is gone!

Babylon represents all these things: the City of Man, godless society, the seduction of affluence and materialism, false religion, the source of persecution for all who seek a better city, the "world." Babylon is a whore, a symbol of the reality that stands behind many earthly expressions. In Nimrod's day, it was the tower of Babel. In Daniel's day, the Babylon of Nebuchadnezzar was the Whore. In John's day, Rome was the Whore. In our day, what might it be--New York, Brussels, Bejing, London? When the final world kingdom emerges, it will be the whore. This world system, with its power, lusts, luxuries and immorality, will be broken and destroyed.

The believer has three enemies in his relationship with God: The devil, the world system, and our own fallen nature. *Revelation* tells us that a day is coming when the devil is going to be totally destroyed. *Revelation* also tells us that a day is coming when we are going to be caught up with Jesus Christ and this earthly body, with its old nature, is going to be changed. We are going to be like Jesus Christ, and we will never again have to fight against that old nature. Finally, *Revelation* tells us that a day is coming when the world system will be destroyed; Babylon the Great will fall! A day is coming when God will destroy every enemy of His people.

Revelation is filled with constant contrasts, constant choices, and constant consequences. No middle ground is ever intended. There are two people groups in the book: the followers of the living God, and the followers of the beast. There are two marks in the book: the mark of the beast and the seal of the living God. There are two cities in the book: Babylon the Whore, and the New Jerusalem, the Bride. In the chapters that follow, the New Jerusalem comes down out of heaven. This is the city whose architect and builder is God. But before the New Jerusalem comes, Jesus Christ returns!

CHAPTER TWENTY: The Return of the King

Hallelujah! For our Lord God Almighty reigns. Let us rejoice and be glad and give him glory! For the wedding of the Lamb has come, and his bride has made herself ready, (Rev. 19:6-7).

Heavenly Hallelujahs

Many of you have probably enjoyed Handel's *Messiah* with its Hallelujah Chorus. You might not be aware that Handel took much the text for the Hallelujah Chorus from *Revelation.* The word "hallelujah" is a Hebrew word. The word only appears in the New Testament four times, and all four of those occurrences are found in *Revelation,* chapter nineteen.

The word is derived from two Hebrew words. The first is the shortened form of the Hebrew name for God: *Yah*. The second is the Hebrew word *halal*, which means "to praise". "Hallelujah" means "praise *YHYH*" or "praise the Lord".

John again sees a scene of tremendous worship in heaven following the destruction of Babylon. If you remember back to the early chapters of *Revelation*, prior to the opening of the seals on the scroll and the beginning of the judgment period, the heavenly scene was filled with worship. John saw all creation worship the one who sat on the throne and the Lamb who was found worthy to take the scroll and open its seals.

By the time we reach this point in *Revelation*, the seals on the scroll have been opened, the trumpets have been sounded, and the bowls have been poured out. Once again, the heavenly scene erupts in worship. Four different times the heavenly multitude shouts out, "Hallelujah!"

Hallelujah! Salvation and glory and power belong to our God, for true and just are his judgments. He has condemned the great prostitute who corrupted the earth by her adulteries. He has avenged on her the blood of his servants, (Rev. 19:1-2).

The first reason for praise is again the destruction of Babylon. The destruction of Babylon not only judges the sin of the world system, it also serves to avenge the martyrdom of those who have paid the ultimate price for their faithfulness.

The elders around the throne join in:

'Halllelujah! The smoke from her goes up for ever and ever,'
(Rev. 19:3).

The second reason for praise is that with the destruction of Babylon, the Kingdom of God will come:

Then I heard what sounded like a great multitude, like the roar of rushing waters and like loud peals of thunder, shouting: 'Hallelujah! For our Lord God Almighty reigns,' (Rev. 19:6).

There are three important Greek words used in the New Testament concerning the reign of Christ and the coming of His kingdom. The first is the Greek word *basileuo,* a verb that means "to reign." This is the word that is used in the above text. The second is the Greek word *basileus,* which is a noun that is translated "King." This word appears a little later in the chapter when Jesus Christ returns and is called "King of Kings." The third is the Greek word *basileia,* which is translated "kingdom." This was the word used earlier when we were told, "The kingdom of the world has become the kingdom of our Lord and of his Christ, and he will reign for ever and ever," (Rev. 11:15).

There is a close connection between these three words. There is a king (*basileus*) who will reign (*basileuo*) in a kingdom (*basileia*). All three of these concepts find their fulfillment here in *Revelation.*

The Kingdom of God

Earlier in *Revelation*, when the seventh trumpet sounded, the following proclamation was made:

The kingdom of the world has become the kingdom of our Lord and of his Christ and he will reign for ever and ever, (Rev. 11:15).

Immediately following this statement, the seventh trumpet sounded. That trumpet ushered in the outpouring of the final seven bowls of God's wrath. With the destruction of Babylon complete, God will establish the consummation of his kingdom on earth.

In the Gospels, Jesus Christ told a series of parables about the "mystery" of the kingdom. This "mystery" is illustrated by an encounter Jesus had with the Pharisees that is recorded in Luke's gospel:

Once, having been asked by the Pharisees when the kingdom of God would come, Jesus replied, 'The kingdom of God does not come visibly, nor will people say, 'Here it is' or 'There it is,' because the kingdom of God is within you, (Luke 17:20).

Jesus was speaking about what some call the mystery form of the kingdom. This dimension of God's kingdom is present wherever God establishes His reign in the hearts of men and women. You and I become citizens of the kingdom of God when we invite Jesus Christ to come into our lives, and ask him to reign over our lives. We become part of the "mystery" form of the kingdom.

This is not a visible, physical kingdom. That is why Jesus Christ could say in Matthew 6:33, "seek first the kingdom of God." He was not telling his disciples to go and look for a geographical area over which God ruled. He was encouraging them to seek first the rule or the reign of God in their lives. That is the mystery form of the kingdom. But the kingdom of God also had a physical expression.

The physical expression of the kingdom of God will be established with the earthly reign of Jesus Christ at his second coming. God promised King David that one of his descendants would sit on the throne of Israel and have an everlasting, eternal kingdom, (II Samuel 7:16). This is why the genealogy of Jesus Christ is traced back to David. One day Christ will establish the kingdom of God in its physical form, and will sit on David's throne. That is what we are talking about when we speak of the *consummation* of the kingdom of God. In our age, there is a *fulfillment* of the coming of the kingdom of God as Christ comes and reigns in our hearts. But in the end-times the kingdom of God will be consummated physically. Jesus Christ will establish his reign on earth.

The Wedding of the Lamb
The third reason for this heavenly chorus of praise is connected to what the text calls "the wedding of the Lamb":

Let us rejoice and be glad and give him glory! For the wedding of the Lamb has come, and his bride has made herself ready...Then the angel said to me, 'Write: Blessed are those who are invited to the wedding supper of the Lamb!' (Rev. 19:7,8).

In the New Testament, several images are used to speak of

145

the relationship between Jesus and his followers. One of the most vivid images is the church as the bride of Christ. The wedding of the Lamb is that point in time when the "bride" is united with Jesus in full consummation.

The Old Testament Jew believed that when Messiah came, there would be a messianic banquet. At this banquet, the Jew would sit at a table and dine with the Messiah. In Isaiah we read:

On this mountain the Lord Almighty will prepare a feast of rich food for all peoples, a banquet of aged wine – the best of meats and the finest of wines, (Isaiah 25:6).

The Jewish people looked forward to this day when Messiah would come and they would attend this banquet. The fulfillment of Isaiah's prophecy occurs in the book of *Revelation*.

The fellowship meal in the oriental culture was a symbol of intimate relationship. The wedding supper of the Lamb occurs at the point in time when the bride of Christ meets the Lord face-to-face, to be with him, forever. This is either a literal feast, where believers, in the presence of God, enjoy a meal; or it is a symbolic way of conveying the truth that believers find their ultimate fulfillment in union with Jesus Christ, enjoying an immediate, first-hand relationship.

Something else transpires somewhere around this point in time. John wrote, "Fine linen, bright and clean, was given her to wear (Fine linen stands for the righteous acts of the saints.)," (Rev. 19:8). Sometime prior to Jesus' second coming, believers will experience a judgment. This is not the Great White Throne judgment of *Revelation,* chapter 20. That judgment involves men and women's eternal destiny. True believers already have their name written in the Book of Life. Their eternal destiny is fixed. But believers have a judgment, also. The apostle Paul wrote:

So we make it our goal to please him, whether we are at home in the body or away from it. For we must all appear before the judgment sent of Christ, that each one may receive what is due him for the things done while in the body, whether good or bad, (II Cor. 5:9, 10).

This is a judgment of faithfulness. Our salvation is not based on our works, but on our relationship with Christ, (Eph. 2:8,9). But we are going to be evaluated by Jesus concerning how we have lived our lives as believers. Christ will reward his faithful followers.

These rewards are related to our role in the age to come. From God's perspective, the most important dimension of our lives is what we do in the age to come. Our focus tends to be so much on this life that we think of heaven and the age to come as a kind of icing on the cake. From God's perspective, this life is like a boot camp, and a testing ground, for what he is going to be able to entrust us with in the age to come. How we spend eternity depends on our faithfulness to God in this life.

In Paul's first letter to Timothy he makes a staggering statement. He exhorts Timothy, "Train yourself to be godly," (I Tim. 4:7). He also gives Timothy the reason for this exhortation: "For physical training is of some value, but godliness has value for all things, holding promise for both the present life and the life to come," (I Tim. 4:8). Somehow, our progress in our relationship with Christ in this age is going to be reflected in the age to come. At the judgment seat of Christ, Christ will judge our faithfulness. We will not be judged for how much we have done or how "great" what we have done seems; rather, the question will be whether or not we have been faithful.

The judgment seat of Christ and the wedding feast of the Lamb are awesome experiences that we have to look forward to when Jesus Christ returns.

The angel instructed John to write: "Blessed are those who are invited to the wedding supper of the Lamb!" (Rev. 19:9). Blessing is that reality which meets the deepest need of the human heart. We have been created with a capacity to experience God's blessing. We might think we desire happiness, but what we really long for is blessing. Happiness is an experience that affects us at the level of the physical, the emotional and the psychological. Blessing affects us at the level of our spirit. When our spirits are blessed, we experience the deepest satisfaction possible. When we stand in the presence of Jesus Christ, we are going to have the deepest needs of the human spirit fully satisfied. That is why David wrote, "In your presence is fullness of joy, and at your right hand are pleasures forevermore," (Ps. 16:11).

The King Comes
I saw heaven standing open and there before me was a white horse,

147

whose rider is called Faithful and True. With justice he judges and makes war. His eyes are like blazing fire, and on his head are many crowns. He has a name written on him that no one but he himself knows. He is dressed in a robe dipped in blood, and his name is the Word of God... On his robe and on his thigh he has this name written: 'KING OF KINGS AND LORD OF LORDS,' (Rev. 19:11-16).

The second coming of Jesus Christ is the hope of every believer. Jesus Christ emphatically taught his personal, physical return. Almost every New Testament book makes reference to the second coming of Jesus Christ. The Apostle Paul wrote to his friend, Titus:

The grace of God that brings salvation has appeared to all men. It teaches us to say no to ungodliness and worldly passions, and to live self-controlled, upright and godly lives in this present age, while we wait for the blessed hope, the glorious appearing of our great God and Savior, Jesus Christ, (Tit. 2:11-13).

To the church at Thessalonica he wrote:

And then the lawless one will be revealed, whom the Lord Jesus will overthrow with the breath of his mouth and destroy by the splendor of his coming, (II Thess. 2:8).

Every chapter of the first letter to the Thessalonians ends with a statement concerning the second coming of Jesus Christ:

Chapter 1, verse 10
To wait for his son from heaven, whom he raised from the dead, Jesus, who rescues us from the coming wrath.

Chapter 2, verse 19
For what is our hope, our joy, or the crown in which we will glory in the presence of our Lord Jesus when he comes. Is it not you?

Chapter 3, verse 13
May he strengthen your hearts so that you may be blameless and holy in the presence of our God and Father, when our Lord Jesus comes with all his holy ones.

Chapter 4, verses 15-18
According to the Lord's own words, we tell you that we who are still alive who are left until the coming of the Lord will certainly not precede those who have fallen asleep. For the Lord himself will come down from heaven, with a loud command, with the voice of the archangel and with the trumpet call of God, and the dead in Christ will rise first. After that we who are still alive and are left will be caught up with them in the clouds to meet the Lord in the air.

Chapter 5, verse 23
May God himself, the God of peace, sanctify you through and through and may your whole spirit, soul and body be kept blameless at the coming of the Lord Jesus Christ.

Jesus himself clearly taught about His second coming:

Do not let your hearts be troubled. Trust in God; trust also in me. In my Father's house are many rooms; if it were not so, I would have told you. I am going there to prepare a place for your. And if I go and prepare a place for you, I will come back and take you to be with me that you also may be where I am, (John 14:1-2).

Matthew recorded Christ's promise:
At that time the sign of the Son of Man will appear in the sky, and all the nations of the earth will mourn. They will see the Son of Man coming on the clouds of the sky, with power and great glory, (Matthew 24:30).

Jesus Christ repeatedly told His disciples, "I am coming again." The big question is not "if", but "when".
Many people have attempted to create a timetable of when that coming will take place. Some use Jesus' Olivet Discourse as evidence that his coming will be in our time. Jesus said:

Now learn this lesson from the fig tree: As soon as its twigs get tender and its leaves come out, you know that summer is near. Even so, when you see all these things, you know that it is near, right at the door. I tell you the truth, this generation will certainly not pass away until all these things have happened. Heaven and earth will pass away, but my words will never pass away, (Matthew 24:32-35).

149

Some prophesy buffs believe that Jesus words about the blooming of the fig tree were fulfilled with the reestablishment of Israel as a nation. They would say that the fig tree "bloomed" on one of two dates. One date would be May 14, 1948, when David Ben Gurion officially declared Israel a nation. Others would point to the Six-day War of 1967, when Israeli soldiers entered the old city of Jerusalem.

Using these dates, they then take Jesus' statement, "I tell you the truth, this generation will certainly not pass away until all these things have happened" to speculate on the date of the return of Jesus. They would say that "this generation" refers to the generation that saw Israel become a nation.

Using forty years as the duration of a biblical generation many predicted that Jesus would return before 1988. That obviously didn't happen. Others, using the 1967 occupation of Jerusalem as the trigger predicted Jesus would come before 2007. Obviously, that didn't happen either.

But what if the fig tree does not represent Israel? Christ might just be using the figure of the fig tree as a analogy to point out that in the same way you know that when a fig tree blossoms, it is going to bear fruit, when you see "all these things happening;" i.e., all the signs he gave in the discourse, then you can know that I'm coming soon.

"This generation" can also mean several things. It could refer to the generation to which he was speaking. In that respect Christ could be talking about the destruction of Jerusalem in 70 A.D., which was part of the prophecy.

But "generation" (genea) can also mean this "race." In other words; Christ might be saying, "The human race will not pass away until what I have said comes true." In that case, the timetables people invent will have no significance at all. The important truth to recognize is that Christ is coming again!

In the Old Testament, Messiah was prophetically pictured in two ways. One the one hand, Messiah was seen as a suffering servant; on the other, as a conquering king. In the oriental world, there were two ways in which a king could come into a territory. He would come in peace, or he could come to wage war. When he came in peace, he rode a donkey. When he came to wage war, he rode a white horse. At the time of Christ's triumphal entry into Jerusalem (Matthew 21:1-11), Jesus rode into Jerusalem on a donkey in fulfillment of the prophecy of Zechariah 9:9:

Rejoice greatly, O Daughter of Zion! Shout, Daughter of Jerusalem! See, your king comes to you, righteous and victorious, lowly and riding on a donkey, on a colt, the foal of a donkey, (Zech. 9:9).

On that first Palm Sunday, Jesus came in peace as a suffering servant. In *Revelation*, he comes riding a white horse. He returns as a conquering king!

The second coming of Christ and the establishment of his kingdom will bring into reality in the time-space continuum the consummation of the kingdom of God on earth. When Christ returns, the prayers of Christians through the centuries are answered: "Your kingdom come: Your will be done on earth as it is in heaven." When we begin to grasp the majesty of this event, we too cry out from our hearts, "*Maranatha*! Come, Lord Jesus!"

And I saw an angel coming down out of heaven, having the key to the Abyss and holding in his hand a great chain. He seized the dragon, that ancient serpent, who is the devil, or Satan, and bound him for a thousand years, (Rev. 20:1-2).

The Millennium

Beginning with chapter twenty of *Revelation*, John was given a vision of the events that will follow the second coming of Jesus Christ. With the fall of Babylon, the world as we know it will come to an end. The godless system that has usurped the rule of God and caused thousands of years of pain and suffering will one day be gone. But the end of the world is the beginning of something so spectacular that even *Revelation* only gives us a few insights into the new beginning. With the return of Jesus Christ, a new world begins. This new world is inaugurated by a transition period of a thousand years. It is called the Millennium.

Historically, there have been three primary ways of understanding what we find in this chapter. Since *Revelation* is highly symbolic, an interpretive decision needs to be made about this thousand-year period. Is it a literal thousand years? Or is it symbolic of something else? The best evidence of what the early church understood about this passage indicates they believed the return of Jesus would be followed by something more along the lines of an actual thousand-year reign of Christ on earth. This understanding has come to be known as Pre-millennialism.

Around the fourth century some interpreters of *Revelation* moved to a more symbolic understanding of what this thousand years represents. Those who believed there was no literal millennium came to be known as amillennialists.

Another later view was the product of an optimistic view of how the church would fulfill its mission in such a way that it would usher in a kind of literal millennium that would be climaxed by the return of Christ. This view is called Postmillennialism.

Why would God design a literal millennium instead of moving directly from the return of Jesus to the new age to come? There are a number of reasons.

The Millennium will be a time when the earth itself will again become what God originally intended it to be. We are told in *Romans* that the entire created universe has suffered the consequences of the Fall, (Rom. 8:20-22). The millennial period is a time when God will restore the earth to its original beauty. The earth will become a paradise once more. Consequently, Isaiah could write of a time when the wolf will lie down with a lamb, and a child will be able to play near the serpent's hole. Nothing will harm or destroy in all of God's new creation. Isaiah wrote that the earth will be filled with the knowledge of the Lord, (Is. 11:6-9).

This will be a unique period in history because it seems to be a time in which immortals and mortals will dwell together on the earth. At this point in time, believers have already been caught up to be with Jesus Christ; they have been transformed; they have received their spiritual bodies; and they have come back with Jesus at the second coming to reign with Christ on earth as immortals. Here in chapter twenty, this is referred to as the first resurrection. John writes:

Blessed and holy are those who share in the first resurrection. The second death has no power over them, but they will be priests of God and of Christ and will reign with him for a thousand years, (Rev. 20:6).

Yet there are also mortals living during the period of time. At the second coming of Christ, national Israel will turn to Jesus as their Messiah, (Zech. 12:10). Perhaps, rather than being changed in the way the believer is when he is caught up to be with Jesus, the Jew who comes to Jesus as Messiah at the second coming will simply live out his or her life as they normally would, and then experience resurrection at the time of normal physical death. This might explain passages such as this, found in Isaiah:

Never again will there be in it an infant who lives but a few days, or an old man who does not live out his years; the one who dies at a hundred will be thought a mere child; the one who fails to reach a hundred will be considered accursed, (Is. 65:20).

There will possibly be people who have not followed the antichrist and have survived the Tribulation. They will come to Israel and worship Jesus. He will reign there as the King over all the earth. This would fill another prophecy of Isaiah:

In the last days the mountain of the Lord's temple will be established as the highest of the mountains; it will be exalted above the hills, and all nations will stream to it, (Is. 2:2).

The Old Testament is filled with many promises to the nation of Israel that have not been fulfilled. Many of these will find their fulfillment during this millennial period. For instance, at the end of the book of *Ezekiel* the prophet sees the Temple rebuilt and the land of Israel resettled. Many of the specifics of Ezekiel's vision go far beyond the restoration that occurred under Ezra and Zerubbabel. Potentially, the Millennium will be a period of time in which both God's original purposes for the earth are realized, and his promises to national Israel are fulfilled.

The Final Test
When the thousand years are over, Satan will be released from his prison and will go out to deceive the nations in the four corners of the earth—Gog and Magog—and to gather them for battle, (Rev. 20:7-8).

At the end of this thousand-year period, Satan will be released. He will be used by God to accomplish the final testing of those mortals who live during the millennial period.

At the end of this short period, those who follow Satan will be destroyed. Finally, Satan will be cast into the lake of fire where Antichrist and the False Prophet have already been thrown. The eternal fate of these three enemies of God is forever sealed: "They will be tormented day and night forever and ever," (Rev. 20:10).

The Final Judgment
Then I saw a great white throne and him who was seated on it. The earth and the heavens fled from his presence, and there was no place for them. And I saw the dead, great and small, standing before the throne, and books were opened. Another book was opened, which is the book of life. The dead were judged according to what they had done as recorded in the books. The sea gave up the dead that were in it, and death and Hades gave up the dead that were in them, and each person was judged according to what they had done, (Rev. 20:11-13).

John saw a great white throne. This will be the place where the final judgment of unredeemed humanity occurs. John saw books

155

opened. He said that everyone who takes part in this judgment will be judged according to what they have done as recorded in these books.

I can imagine that one of these books contains the Law of God. The Law is the perfect standard for how a man or woman would have to live to be declared righteous on the basis of their own works. We might think of the second book as containing the record of the lives of every man and woman who has ever lived. Imagine these two books being compared. In other words, apart from the gift of grace and salvation found in Jesus, men and women will be judged by how their lives stack up against God's standards. If anyone's life has perfectly conformed to God's standards then they can enter the kingdom without depending on the saving work of Jesus Christ. No one will be found who passes this test. This is where the third book comes into play.

The third book that is opened is the Book of Life. This is a book that records the names of all who possess spiritual life through faith in Jesus Christ. In his first letter to the churches of Asia Minor, John had previously written:

He who has the Son has life; he who does not have the Son of God does not have life, (I Jn. 5:12).

The indwelling presence of Jesus Christ in our lives guarantees that our name will be written in the Book of Life.

Hell
If anyone's name was not found written in the Book of Life, he was thrown into the lake of fire, (Rev. 20:15).

The lake of fire is the eternal destiny of anyone whose name is not found written in this third book. Jesus frequently spoke of a place he described as the "outer darkness", where there would be "weeping and gnashing of teeth". Five times in Matthew's gospel alone Jesus referred to this place as the final destination of the unrighteous.

Several Greek words are used in the New Testament to refer to this spiritual reality. It is sometimes referred to by the use of the word *Hades*. In the Jewish conception of the afterlife, the departed spirits of the dead went to a place called Sheol. Sheol was divided into two compartments. There was a place in Sheol where the souls of the departed unrighteous dwelled; and there was a place in Sheol where the souls of the departed righteous dwelled. The place reserved for the righteous was called Abraham's Bosom, or Paradise. The place for the departed unrighteous was called Hades. When Jesus rose from the dead and ascended to the Father, Paradise was emptied and the righteous ascended with Jesus to be with him forever. In *Revelation*, we are told that Hades will also be "emptied". But it will be consumed by the lake of fire, which is called the second death.

The most common word used in the New Testament to speak of hell is the Greek word Gehenna. This word actually comes from the Hebrew word *Gehennom*, which means "Valley of Hinnom". Gehenna is pictured in the Bible as a place of fiery, eternal punishment. Gehenna is probably the equivalent of the lake of fire in *Revelation*. The Valley of Hinnom was the trash dump outside of Jerusalem where a fire was continually kept burning. The garbage from Jerusalem was burned in this fire. This became a graphic picture of hell for the Jew living around Jerusalem. What is hell like? It is a place where immortal souls become like garbage burning in a trash dump for all eternity. This is the sobering imagery used to describe the afterlife of the unrighteous.

Hell was not designed for human beings. Hell was a place God designed for Satan and the fallen angles. Jesus said:

Then he will say to those on his left, 'Depart from me, you who are accursed, into the eternal fire prepared for the devil and his angels,' (Mt. 25:41).

There is a sense in which God never sends anyone to hell. We make our own choice. God did not design hell for people, but people have been given the freedom to make an eternal choice. If they choose to reject Jesus Christ, they then will experience the second death, which is the lake of fire.

The formula is really quite simple. If you are born once, you die twice. But if you are born twice, you only have to die once. If you are born only once (physically), you die physically, and at the judgment, you die eternally. But if you are born physically and then born again spiritually, the only death you will experience is physical death. Physical death for the believer is a door opening

157

to eternal life.

Revelation clearly affirms the message of the New Testament: no one, on the basis of their own works, will be found worthy to be part of the Kingdom of God. The choice is ours. We can spend eternity with Satan and his angels in the lake of fire; like the garbage dump outside of Jerusalem. Or we can spend eternity with Jesus Christ in the New Jerusalem that he has prepared for those who choose him. The first destination is the choice of rebellious humanity. The second is the gift of a gracious God. The man or woman whose name is found written in the Book of Life has passed their final exams. God has something beyond our ability to comprehend awaiting them.

CHAPTER TWENTY-TWO: *All Things New*

Then I saw a new heaven and a new earth, for the first heaven and the first earth had passed away, and there was no longer any sea, (Rev. 21:1).

At the end of the vision of the thousand year earthly reign of Christ, John saw a vision of a new heaven and a new earth. He wrote that "the first earth had passed away." In one of his other letters to the churches of Asia Minor John had written, "The world and its desires pass away, but the man who does the will of God lives forever," (I John 2:17). At this point in *Revelation*, John saw what will happen when that old order of things actually passes away. He saw a new heaven and a new earth that contained a New Jerusalem.

The New Jerusalem

I saw the Holy City, the New Jerusalem, coming down out of heaven from God, prepared as a bride beautifully dressed for her husband, (Rev. 21:2).

This new heaven and new earth are characterized by a city, the New Jerusalem. As with almost every other symbol we have studied in *Revelation,* there is more than one opinion about the New Jerusalem. It could be a literal city, or it might symbolize the people of God in their glorified state. The New Jerusalem, the city of God's people, is referred to as a bride. This metaphor is used throughout the New Testament in relationship to Jesus and the church. Perhaps the best way to express what the New Jerusalem represents would be to say that it is a picture of God's people in their eternal dwelling place.

Several characteristics of the New Jerusalem are pointed out in this passage. The most important characteristic is that God dwells there. A loud voice cries out, "Now the dwelling of God is with men, and he will live with them," (Rev. 21:3). In the New Jerusalem, there will no longer be a secondhand experience of God, but rather, the direct experience of the presence of God in our midst. This direct presence of God changes many of the dimensions of life in "the old order." In this city there will be no more sorrow, death, sickness, pain, or sin, (Rev. 21:4). Here men will experience perfect fellowship with God and with each other.

159

Scientists tell us that currently people use less than 10% of their brain's capacity. Everything that we experience in life, we experience with only a small percentage of our brain's potential. When we enter the presence of Jesus, we will be transformed and given new bodies. When sin is no longer a part of our nature, perhaps God will give us the use of the other 90% of our brain.

Think about the best experiences you have had in your life; the times when you were experiencing another person's love, the warmth of caring relationships, or the beauty of sensing God's presence. We experience all of these with the use of only 10% of our brain. What would it be like to multiply the intensity of the enjoyment and satisfaction of life's most meaningful experiences by 900%? Perhaps that is one small blessing we have to look forward to when the old order passes away and God says, "I'm making everything new!" (Rev. 21:5).

If this is a literal city, the dimensions are staggering. It is either a cube or a pyramid that is fifteen hundred miles by fifteen hundred miles by fifteen hundred miles. We might think of it as a city spanning from Denver to Los Angeles, and from Canada to the Gulf of Mexico. Now take that area and cube it! When Jesus said, "In my Father's house there are many rooms (John 14:2), he wasn't kidding! If this is a literal city, it is immense! As the old adage goes, "There is a room at the top."

The gates of the city bear the names of the twelve tribes of Israel: God's Old Testament people. The foundations of the city are inscribed with the names of the twelve apostles: God's New Testament people. This is a place in which the people of God throughout all the ages will dwell.

The building materials of the city are precious stones, pearls, and gold. In "Babylon," men sold their souls and rejected God for gold, silver and precious stones. In the age to come, those items are so insignificant that they are used like asphalt, bricks and concrete.

Have you ever wondered why men and women desire material possessions? We desire cars, or houses, or clothes, or jewels because of the pleasure these items bring us. For some of us, playing golf gives pleasure. For some, riding a motorcycle gives pleasure. God has created us with a healthy capacity to experience pleasure and enjoyment. If you get down to the root of all this, it is not the material things or experiences that we desire; it is the joy or pleasure that these particular things give us. Now, take your healthy capacity for pleasure and enjoyment, and increase that capacity by 900%. Then ponder the possibility that in the age to come, God is going to totally fill that capacity, and that he won't need a single material possession to do it! God will be able to totally fill that capacity for pleasure through our relationship with Him!

Think of the greatest spiritual experience you have ever had: the time when you felt emotionally and spiritually the closest to God that you have ever felt. Now, multiply that experience by 900%. David called it "fullness of joy". He said that is found in God's presence, (Psalm 16:11). That is what God is going to give us in the age to come. We cannot begin to conceive of the beauty and excitement of what God has planned for us in the New Jerusalem. As the Apostle Paul said, "No eye has ever seen, no ear has heard, no mind has conceived what God has prepared for those who love him," (I Cor. 2:9).

No Temple
I did not see a temple in the city, because the Lord God Almighty and the Lamb are its temple, (Rev. 21:22).

Something is missing in the New Jerusalem. It is a city without a temple. The Temple was the place of contact with God. Jews, prior to 70 A.D. would go to the Temple in Jerusalem to be near God's presence. There in the Holy of Holies, a small thirty by thirty foot room, God revealed His glory. But only the High Priest, on the Day of Atonement, was able to enter this room and stand in the presence of God's glory. *Revelation* tells us that in the age to come, there is going to be a fifteen hundred mile by fifteen hundred mile by fifteen hundred mile Holy of Holies! God's presence will perfectly permeate the entire city so that everyone will dwell in the "Holy of Holies", in continual contact with the presence of God.

In the last fifty years there has been a shift of emphasis in the Christian church. There was a time when Christianity heavily emphasized the reality of heaven. In the last fifty years there has been a strong emphasis on the present realities of the Christian life. I have heard many people say that the Christian life is so meaningful that it is worth being a Christian even if we had nothing to look forward to after death. But we have lost sight of the importance of what God has planned for us in the age to come. What God has prepared for us in the life to come is worth any sacrifice we need to make to walk faithfully with Him in this life.

The River of Life
Then the angel showed me the river of the water of life, as clear as crystal, flowing from the throne of God and of the Lamb down the middle of the great street of the city, (Rev. 22:1,2).

The message of the Bible from *Genesis* through *Revelation* is a message of life and death. In the early chapters of this book we discussed the words that are used in the New Testament to speak about life. The Greek word *psuche* speaks of the physical life that all living beings possess. The Greek word *zoe* speaks of the uncreated spiritual life that comes from God and becomes ours when we are born-again of the Spirit. In *Genesis*, God created man to possess this spiritual life. This *zoe* life, which was given in *Genesis* was lost at the Fall.

Jesus came to make it possible for us to once again possess this life. The Bible says, "In him was life (zoe)," (John 1:4). Jesus is the source of spiritual life. Because of the death and the resurrection of Jesus Christ, it is possible for men and women to once again possess *zoe*, the spiritual life that comes from God. In *Revelation* two pictures are given concerning this spiritual life.

There is a river of living water flowing through the New Jerusalem. John wrote both *Revelation* and the *Gospel of John*. He used a series of identical Greek words in *John* chapter seven and *Revelation* chapter twenty-two. In *John*, Jesus stood in the middle of a feast in Jerusalem and made this claim:

If a man is thirsty, let him come to me and drink. Whoever believes in me, as the Scripture has said, rivers of living water will flow from within him, (John 7:37,38).

John commented that this statement referred to the Holy Spirit who would be given when Jesus was once again glorified. The outpouring of the Spirit on the day of Pentecost was a sign that Jesus had been glorified with the glory he possessed from all eternity and relinquished during his incarnation.

The same words used in *John* are now used in *Revelation* where in the New Jerusalem a river flows "from the throne of God and of the Lamb," (Rev. 22:1). It is called "the river of the water of life (zoe)." In the age to come there will be a continual, increasing manifestation of the Holy Spirit available to the resident of the New Jerusalem. What was lost in the Garden, and made possible again by what Jesus did at the cross, is now fully experienced in the New Jerusalem.

The Tree of Life
On each side of the river stood the tree of life, bearing twelve crops of fruit, yielding its fruit every month. And the leaves of the tree are for the healing of the nations, (Rev. 22:2).

The imagery of the tree of life immediately takes us back to *Genesis*. In *Genesis* we are told what conditions were like in the Garden of Eden before sin entered God's creation:

And the Lord God made all kinds of trees grow out of the ground-- trees that were pleasing to the eye and good for food. In the middle of the garden were the tree of life and the tree of the knowledge of good and evil, (Genesis 2:9).

The tree of life was available to Adam and Eve. They could have eaten from it and lived forever. After they sinned, by eating from the tree of the knowledge of good and evil, God made the following decision:

And the Lord God said, 'The man has now become like one of us, knowing good and evil. He must not be allowed to reach out his hand and take also from the tree of life, and eat, and live forever,' (Gen. 3:22).

God banished Adam and Eve from Eden. The tree of life was no longer accessible...till now! This was an act of grace that kept a fallen humanity from living forever. But in the New Jerusalem, that which was lost in *Genesis* is given again in *Revelation*. There is perfect harmony from *Genesis* through *Revelation*. Access to the tree of life, lost in the Garden, and provided for at the cross, is now made available in the New Jerusalem.

The Curse
No longer will there be any curse, (Rev. 22:3).

In *Genesis*, humanity chose sin. Grave consequences

accompanied that choice. The suffering, struggle, and evil in the world today are all results of the curse that came as a result of sin. In *Revelation* that curse is permanently removed. Christ paid the price for that to happen. In *Galatians* we are told:

Christ redeemed us from the curse of the law by becoming a curse for us, for it is written: 'Cursed is everyone who is hung on a tree,' (Gal. 3:13).

That which Christ accomplished at Calvary is fully realized in the New Jerusalem.

Face to Face
They will see his face, (Rev. 22:4).

God created us so he could enjoy "face-to-face" fellowship with us. In *Genesis*, we are given a picture of God walking in the garden in the cool of the day, coming to meet with Adam. Once the Fall took place, Adam no longer enjoyed that kind of fellowship with God. Again, because of what Jesus did on the cross, the potential for that kind of fellowship has been restored. But it will not be fully realized until the age to come. Then we will see him "face-to-face." We will be able to stand in his presence, touch him, talk with him, and have perfect fellowship with him. This is the greatest promise of *Revelation*! What a beautiful picture God paints. All that man lost in the garden, and which Christ paid for at Calvary, will be fully realized in the New Jerusalem. Those who know Jesus have a fantastic new world to look forward to, and to enjoy forever!

CHAPTER TWENTY-THREE: *The final invitation*

The angel said to me, 'These words are trustworthy and true. The Lord, the God of the spirits of the prophets, sent his angel to show his servants the things that must soon take place,' (Rev. 22:6).

The Journey Reviewed

We have been on quite a journey together as we have studied the pages of *Revelation*. Let's go back and take a bird's eye view of where we have come from:

Chapter 1

The year was 95 A.D. John was a political prisoner on the island of Patmos. He was there because he had refused to worship Caesar and instead had pledged his allegiance to Jesus Christ. There on the Island of Patmos he received an *apocalupsis*, a "revelation," an "unveiling." It was a revelation concerning the future, and the control of the future by Jesus Christ. John received this revelation by means of a vision about the things "soon to take place."

The revelation begins with a vision of the risen, glorified, and exalted Christ. He stands in the midst of seven candlesticks. They are symbols of the church. This vision symbolizes that the glorified Christ is the Lord of the church. Jesus dictated seven letters that John was to send to seven churches. Those letters are contained in the following two chapters.

Chapters 2-3

Seven letters are addressed to seven first-century churches. The messages of these seven letters concern the spiritual state of each of the churches. Jesus tells them what he likes, what he doesn't like, what they need to do about what he doesn't like, and what they have to look forward to in the coming new age if they do what he tells them to do. Seven times Jesus challenges believers to be faithful in the present, in light of the future.

Chapters 4-5

In chapters 4-5, John is given a second vision of Jesus Christ. He is caught up into heaven and sees the throne of God. A scroll appears. That scroll contains the events of the final years of human history. A voice cries out, "Who is worthy to take the scroll and to open its seals?" No one was found who was worthy.

Suddenly, Christ appears. He appears as a Lamb who was slain but is alive: perfect in power and wisdom. The risen Christ is Lord of heaven. Christ takes the scroll. Voices cry out, "Worthy is the Lamb." Christ begins to open the scroll.

Chapter 6

The period of the Tribulation begins. The Tribulation contains three sets of seven judgments covering chapters 6-18. In chapter 6, Christ opens six seals. The six seals produce a time of partial judgment.

Chapter 7

After the six seals are opened, a critical question is asked: "Who can stand?" Who can survive the end of the world? In chapter 7 the answer to this question is given. 144,000 "Jews" are sealed, and a great multitude stands before the throne in heaven. In a symbolic vision, John is shown those who will be protected from the wrath of God during the Tribulation. Who can survive? The men and women who are "sealed for survival."

Chapters 8-9

The seventh seal is opened. Seven angels are given seven trumpets. Chapters 8 and 9 contain the trumpet judgments. The seals introduced partial judgment. When the trumpets sound, judgment intensifies. Again, the question could be asked, "Who can survive?" The next five chapters contain the answer.

Chapter 10-11

Chapters 10 and 11 contain visions of a scroll, a temple, and two witnesses. In another symbolic vision John is shown the ministry of the church during the tribulation as God's witnesses to the world. They are "measured" for protection. When martyred, they are resurrected and caught up to heaven.

Chapters 12-14

Chapters 12-14 contain a panorama of world history from a spiritual perspective. A dragon pursues a woman. Satan attempts to destroy the people of God. There is war in heaven. Satan is cast down to earth and the full power of his evil is unleashed through the beast: the Antichrist. Antichrist heads a one world political-economic system. The false prophet seduces men to worship

166

Antichrist. Those who remain faithful to Christ stand victorious with the Lamb on the Heavenly Mt. Zion.

Chapters 15-18
In chapters 15 and 16 the final judgment of God is executed on an unbelieving world. The seven bowls of God's wrath are poured out. Chapters 17 and 18 contain the destruction of Babylon. God destroys the godless world system. Who can survive the end of the "world?" The following chapters reaffirm the answer to this question.

Chapters 19-20
In chapter 19 Christ returns. Those men and women who have committed their lives to him accompany him. They are his called, chosen, and faithful followers. The marriage supper of the Lamb is followed by the return of Jesus Christ at the battle of Armageddon. The False Prophet and Antichrist are defeated and thrown into the lake of fire. Satan is bound. Christ establishes His millennial kingdom. Satan is released, defeated, and cast into the lake of fire. Finally, the unbelieving world is judged before the Great White Throne.

Chapters 21-22
In chapters 21 and 22, John is given the final vision of Jesus Christ. This vision concerns Christ and the age to come. Christ is not only Lord of the church; not only Lord of heaven; not only Lord of earth: he is Lord of the entire universe. In chapter 21, we see the new heaven and the new earth; the old order has passed away; everything is made new. A New Jerusalem descends from God. It is the "bride" of the Lamb. In this city there is perfect fellowship with God: fullness of joy and pleasures forevermore.

In light of all that He has revealed to John in this "unveiling" on the Island of Patmos, Jesus Christ issues a final invitation.

The Final Invitation
The Spirit and the bride say, 'Come!' And let him who hears say, 'Come!' Whoever is thirsty, let him come; and whoever wishes, let him take the free gift of the water of life, (Rev. 22:17).

Revelation ends with an invitation. It is an invitation to take a drink of the water of life. The invitation reminds us that when the world's menu leaves us thirsting for something more, we may come to the river of God and drink of Jesus Christ. We may drink freely and we may drink deeply. Man can enter into a vital relationship with God. The Spirit and the Bride say, "Come!"

The first message of the Bible is that man was created to have fellowship with God. When man fell, that fellowship was broken. At the cross, all that was necessary for that fellowship to be restored was accomplished by Jesus Christ. The last message of the Bible is that God, once again, is inviting us to have fellowship with him. "Come!" That "come" is the beckoning call of the great lover of our souls. His greatest desire is that we live in a love relationship with him: a relationship in which we allow him to express his great love for us and we reciprocate with our love.

Finally, Jesus Christ says, "Yes, I am coming soon," (Rev. 22:20). The book began with the exclamation, "Look, he is coming with the clouds," (Rev. 1:7). The book ends with the proclamation, "Yes, I am coming soon!" Jesus is coming again. The message of *Revelation* is really quite simple: Jesus Christ is Lord of the church: therefore, as part of the church, you and I are called to a faithful relationship with Him. Jesus Christ is Lord of heaven: the future is in his hands. Jesus Christ is Lord of earth: he is coming again to establish his kingdom on earth. Jesus Christ is Lord of the universe: in the age to come, Christ will reign. Jesus Christ: Lord of the church, Lord of heaven, Lord of earth, and Lord of the universe. With the Apostle John, we proclaim, "Amen, Come Lord Jesus."

The grace of the Lord Jesus be with God's people. Amen, (Rev. 22:21).

What in the World is Going On?

In *Revelation Explained*, Dr. Bob Beltz answers this critical question. Unpacking the message of the book of Revelation in an intelligent and yet intelligible way, Dr. Beltz explains God's plan for the future of the human race.

Bob Beltz is the Senior Pastor of Highline Community Church in Denver, Colorado. He is also the President of The Telos Project, a Christian non-profit ministry working to communicate the message of the Bible through print, television, film, and social media in culturally relevant ways. He is the author of fourteen books, including the best-selling *Walk Like a Man*, and the novels *Somewhere Fast*, and *She Loves You*. Bob has worked as a consultant and associate producer on over twenty major films including *The Lion, the Witch, and the Wardrobe*, *Amazing Grace*, *The Chronicles of Narnia: Prince Caspian*, *The Voyage of the Dawn Treader*, and *Son of God*. He was an associate producer of the Emmy nominated *The Bible* series on the History Channel.

Dr. Beltz earned his masters and doctoral degrees from Denver Seminary. Bob and his wife Allison have been married for over forty years. They have two children, Stephanie and Baker, and three grandchildren, Olivia, Jaxon, and Emma.

If you only read one book this year, this is the book!